D1538873

www.imaging

ROBIN NICHOLS AND PHILIP ANDREWS

SERIES CONSULTANT
ALASTAIR CAMPBELL

WATSON-GUPTILL
PUBLICATIONS
New York

First published in the
United States in 2002 by
Watson-Guptill
Publications, a division of
VNU Business Media, Inc.,
770 Broadway,
New York, NY 10003

The information
contained in this book is
given without warranty
and, while every
precaution has been
taken in compiling the
book, neither the author
nor the publisher
assumes any
responsibility or liability
whatsoever to any
person or entity with
respect to any errors
that may exist in the
book, nor for any loss
of data that may occur
as the result of such
errors or for the
efficacy or performance
of any product or
process described in
the book.

This book was
conceived, designed
and produced by:
The Ilex Press Ltd
The Barn
College Farm
1 West End
Whittlesford
Cambridge
CB2 4LX

Sales Office
The Old Candlemakers
West Street, Lewes
East Sussex
BN7 2NZ

Publisher:
Sophie Collins
Art Director:
Alastair Campbell
Editorial Director:
Steve Luck
Design Manager:
Tony Seddon
Project Editor:
Rowan Davies
Designers:
Jane and Chris Lanaway

www.designdirectories.com

ISBN 0-8230-5855-7

Library of Congress
Cataloging-in-Publication
Data

Nichols, Robin, 1955–
   www.imaging / Robin
Nichols & Philip Andrews.
   p. cm. — (Design
directories)
   ISBN 0-8230-5855-7
      1. Web sites–Design.
      2. Computer
         graphics.
      I. Andrews, Philip,
1964– II. Title. III. Series.
   TK5105.888 .N483 2002
   005.7'2—dc21
            2001008608

Originated and printed
by Hong Kong Graphics
and Printing Ltd, China

All Web sites mentioned
in this book were current
at the time of writing, but
due to the changing
nature of the Internet, it
is possible that some are
no longer in existence or
that the URLs listed are
now hosting different
content. The authors and
publisher cannot accept
liability for these changes
and apologize for any
inconvenience.

CONTENTS

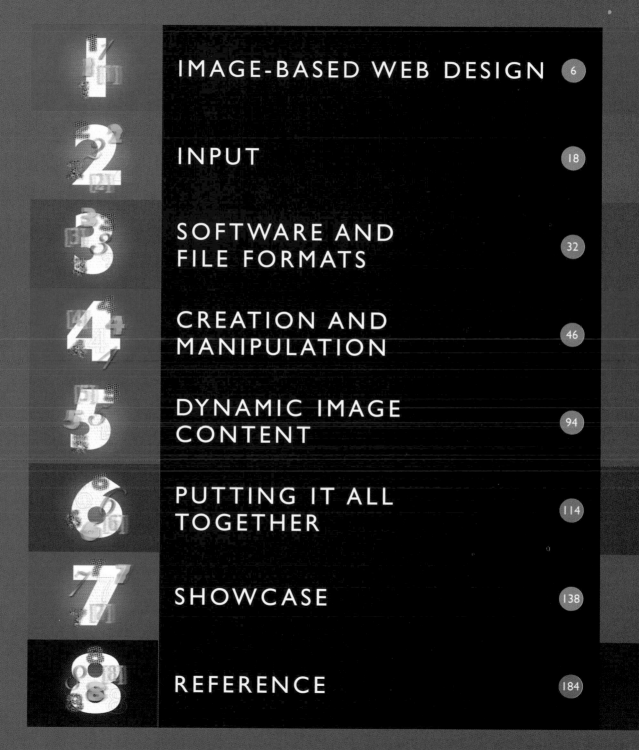

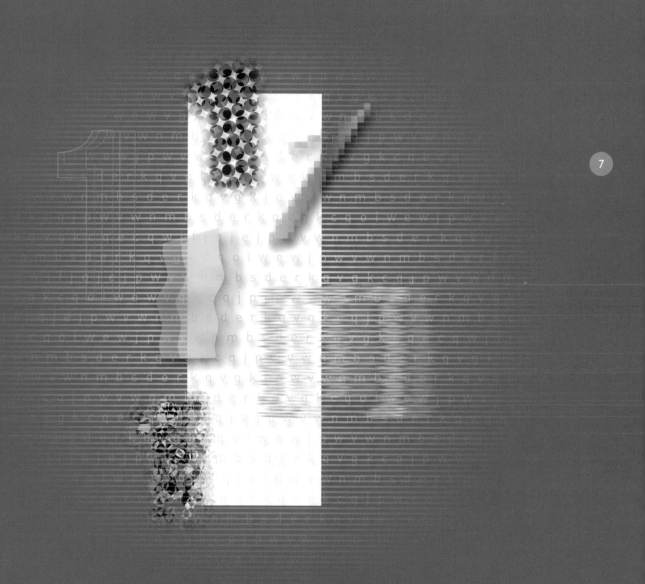

DIFFERENCES BETWEEN PRINT AND THE WEB

Web designers will be immediately aware of the huge differences between the Web and print; they are "differences" because not all of them are advantages. For example, though a Web site might cost less to develop compared with an equivalent print product, it certainly doesn't have the traditional and physical reassurances of a beautifully printed book or magazine.

However, publishing on the Internet offers some irresistible advantages over print. To begin with, publishing costs on the Internet are generally less expensive compared with print. While designing a Web site might take just as much time and money as it would for an equivalent print project, there are no further costs to face once it's done (except perhaps for paying an ISP to host it). Publishing on the Web means that distribution is taken care of, the "print run" is infinite and, unlike print, you can be as lavish as you want with color on the Web and not worry about paying extra. Unlike print content, Web content can be updated immediately and consistently at very little cost.

The Web is much more than a text and image medium; content can include animation, video, and sound. The technology involved also means that businesses and other groups can get instant feedback when working via the Internet, and so discover the preferences of visitors. This is not to say that print hasn't got a lot to offer—in fact print trumps the Web on a number of fronts. For instance, print operates at higher resolutions and unless you're really cutting costs, images will always look better on paper. Print is a robust medium; it can be read anywhere and is not subject to the technical failures of the Internet. There are far more readers in the world than there are Internet users and even the most dedicated fan of the Web would agree that reading long passages of text on screen can be tiring. Also, the Web is a new medium and for the foreseeable future people will be more inclined to trust the printed word over what they read online.

To a Web designer attempting to plan a brilliant career, the advantages of print might appear daunting, which is why it's important to learn the tricks of the imaging trade. Without these it is not possible to work on the Web and stay in front.

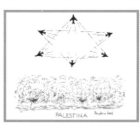

1 | 2

How the *La Stampa* newspaper of Turin, Italy, covered the news on December 4, 2001 in its Internet and print editions. From a design point of view the print edition probably has the upper hand; the design area is so much larger, typography can be employed in far more subtle ways than HTML text can ever allow, and photographs can be used without regard for download times. However, the newspaper can never compete with the interactive features of the Web site edition, including archive searches and a Lira/Euro conversion calculator. Also, the Web site need never be out of date, which is a distinct advantage when the task is communicating news.

THE AESTHETICS OF COLOR

As with the subtle balance of space and images, colors used within a Web site can have a big influence on the feel of your site. Colors are closely associated with mood, such as passionate reds, calming greens, and serious grays. Link the content to the color—look at the product and find a color to suit. This might be as subtle as coordinating the color of text headers or it might be something a little more direct, for example linking the design with the hues and saturation from the products posted on the site.

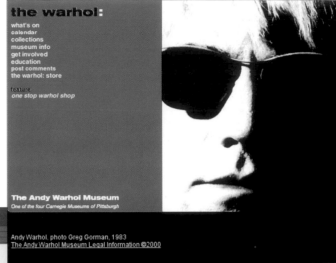

10

1
The Warhol Web site uses a classic two-tone photo of Andy Warhol to provide the visual draw to its site. Although there's no real detail in the picture, the symbolism presented by this image is hard to miss, especially as it is presented in such bold color—typical of the artist himself.

2 | 3
Sony's German site reflects the mood of the product—high tech and stylish. It is beautifully designed with easy navigation and its clean use of color neither overpowers nor dominates the product focus.

4
Digital photography studio Red Rocket demands attention with its aggressive use of a blood red background fill on every page.

5
US-based Crayola has a site that exemplifies just how much fun you can have using heavy colors and textures on the Web. At first appearance, this looks more like a kids' site: it's very busy and is packed with items of visual interest. The crayons, of course, make natural navigation buttons and the scribbling a perfect, colorful background. The designers have (sensibly) left the copy on a single-color platform above the background to retain its legibility. This is an obvious design requirement that many other designers forget to do—with the result that the site becomes hard to read.

USING PICTORIAL SYMBOLISM/BRANDING

The World Wide Web is a visual medium. That is to say people are generally unwilling to read long passages of text on screen, and instead use the visuals as a way of gathering information. Therefore, to create an effective Web site you have to communicate with it pictorially. Finding or creating images that relate specifically to a site is a good way to induce the casual surfer to extend his or her visit, and then to have the viewer remember what was seen there.

Photographers might typically go for something that looks like film when putting a site together. Sprocket holes arranged down the side of a page is an obvious visual metaphor for this type of application. Well-worked maybe, but this metaphor still evokes a strong sense of what the site is about.

12

1

www.mgm.com shows not only its trademark roaring lion logo but it also uses the symbolism of film sprocket holes to denote its movies.

2

The Australian-based consumer retail chain Target uses a target symbol to denote its range of products in its TV ads. The site continues with this metaphor, using the target circle in a number of guises to add to its corporate identity.

3

www.homebrewing.com There's nothing wrong with going for an obvious symbol for a site, provided it's a strong and simple one.

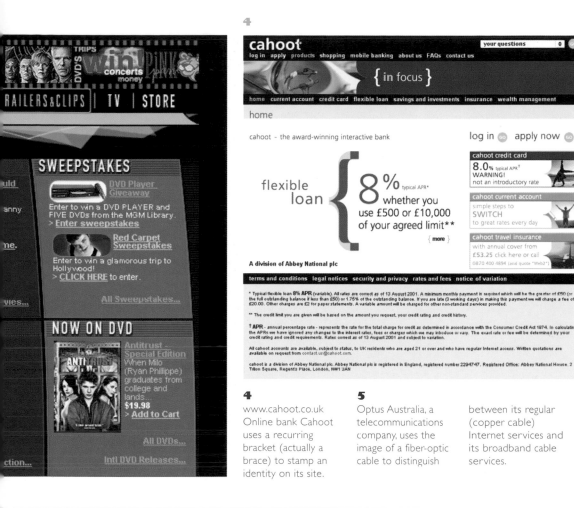

4

4
www.cahoot.co.uk
Online bank Cahoot
uses a recurring
bracket (actually a
brace) to stamp an
identity on its site.

5
Optus Australia, a
telecommunications
company, uses the
image of a fiber-optic
cable to distinguish

between its regular
(copper cable)
Internet services and
its broadband cable
services.

Of course a metaphor such as the sprocket holes could also be misconstrued as representing a film company, a movie production house, or a picture library, so it is worthwhile considering all the possible interpretations of your chosen metaphor before you commit to it.

A fine example of a visual symbol is pictured here—the business of a local home-brewing supplier. As a business involved in such a trade, this US-based company chose to use a photograph of a bottle and glass of beer to run as part of the masthead, its main identifying logo. Wherever the users see this logo, they know they are in the same home-brewing site. Refining this symbolism a little further, the body copy is separated into sections using an image of a stalk of barley.

13

ABOUT WEB COLOR I

Color fidelity is the biggest challenge in commercial graphics reproduction. The issue boils down to the difference between color space, being a theoretical definition of color variance, and device "gamut," being the actual range of colors achievable by that device whether it's a printer, monitor, scanner, and so on.

For Web design, the most commonly used color spaces for everyday onscreen work are red-green-blue (RGB) and hue-saturation-lightness/brightness (HSL or HSB). Both systems define millions of different colors within the 24-bit or 36-bit restriction of professional computer monitors and graphics cards. But variances in screen technology, the power regulation in the unit, and even the quality of the phosphors in a conventional CRT monitor will affect how the colors are reproduced.

A print designer can compensate for these differences by installing a color management system, with the ultimate color intent being the final printing press. A Web designer's color intent, however, is effectively the billions of potential Internet users all over the world. You have no control over how these people have set up their monitors, what the ambient lighting is, or what their color capability might be. But what you can do is stay aware of certain fundamental issues that affect Web graphics across different technologies.

To start with, you can't assume that all Web visitors enjoy the luxury of your 36-bit graphics card and calibrated studio monitor. There remain millions of Web users out there with only 256-color (8-bit) graphics capability—or even less in certain mobile devices. It's not necessary to aim at the lowest common denominator as it was in the mid-1990s, but nor do you want your Web site to look terrible on certain computer screens because of unpredictable color downsampling.

For this reason, most Web browsers support a special color palette of 216 specific hues and shades. This allows breathing room for each computing platform's

1

This image was prepared on a PC running Windows. But here it is viewed in a Web browser on a Mac, where the different default screen display has the effect of making the image appear paler than it should.

1

2

2

So we reopened the picture on the Mac and adjusted it to the correct monitor settings. Having made the adjustment, here's how the result appeared when viewed back on the PC: too dark. There's no immediate solution; it's up to you to find a compromise between the two platform gammas.

14

3 | 4

Your original image might appear perfect when viewed on screen in millions or even just thousands of colors, but dropping down to an unpredictable 256-color palette space can produce appalling visual artifacts.

own "system" colors, while guaranteeing a certain predictability for the images themselves from one computer to another. These 216 colors are often known as the "Web color space" or "Web-safe colors."

You should also be aware that different platforms employ different monitor setups. In particular, Mac users tend to have their monitors set to a gamma of 1.8 while Windows users have theirs defaulting to 2.2. Graphics prepared on a Mac will look dark when viewed on a Windows computer, and those prepared under Windows will look pale on a Mac. There's nothing you can do about this other than to avoid using very dark and very pale colors at the onset.

15

5

The obvious solution is to convert the image to a 256-color file format such as GIF, shown here in detail using Mac system colors.

6

But now compare it with the same image converted to Windows system colors. There are subtle and not-so-subtle differences to take into account.

7

The compromise solution is to apply the cross-platform, cross-browser set of 216 Web-safe colors. It's not a perfect result by any means, but at least it's predictable and fixed.

5

6

7

ABOUT WEB COLOR 2

Web color space is not the same as print color space. It is smaller, less subtle, and often unpredictable. However, if you want your Web site to work for as wide an audience as possible, it's all you have to play with—at least for the time being.

Because reducing a continuous-tone photograph to less than 256 colors is so limiting, Photoshop and a number of other image-preparation software packages offer the designer a number of dithering options that reduce the noticeable image degradation. Dithering is a software process that attempts to re-create a color or

1 | 2 | 3

Dithering attempts to smooth out the color shortcomings experienced with Indexed Color. However, it also makes files larger and this will have a negative effect on its ultimate download speed when rapid access to illustrations is of prime importance.

4

If you are not happy with the results from Photoshop's pre-set dithering, you can make your own with its supplied DitherBox technology.

GIF
46.3K
17 sec @ 28.8Kbps

100% dither
Perceptual palette
32 colors

1

GIF
54.74K
20 sec @ 28.8Kbps

100% dither
Perceptual palette
32 colors

2

GIF
32.33K
12 sec @ 28.8Kbps

0% dither
Perceptual palette
32 colors

3

tone by placing other colors in close proximity to each other to simulate that color or tone. Although it's quite effective, dithering does increase the size of image files and thus slows transmission and download times. If you are trying to shave every last kilobyte off your page, don't dither if you can avoid it. Dithering options include: diffusion, pattern, and noise. The differences between these three dithering methods are extremely slight, though "diffusion" usually provides the most effective solution to dithering problems.

Dithering is also applied to color when displayed on computers with limited color capabilities. This is known as browser dithering. Designers don't have to work blind when dithering—the effects can be previewed in the designer's own browser by setting the color display to 256 colors and launching the file directly into the browser.

Reducing files in color and size further requires the use of specialized optimization. These techniques are discussed in greater detail in Section Three.

17

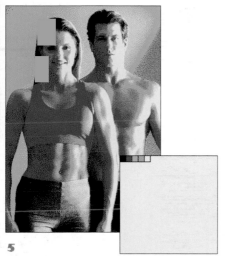

5

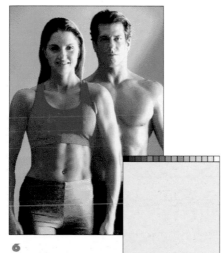

6

7

8

9

5 | 6 | 7 | 8
GIF files can be optimized to contain 256 colors or only two, depending on the color makeup and the designer's intent. This is a continuous-tone image converted from RGB to a Compuserve GIF file with 5, 16, 32, 64, 126, and 216 colors respectively. No dither was applied.

18

SCANNERS

3

The simplest and cheapest way of transferring images onto your computer is to use a flatbed scanner. This device comprises a glass plate—the bed—under which a scanning head moves along a precision track. Inside the scanning head is an array of CCDs (charged coupled devices), tiny light-sensitive devices that produce electrical signals in response to the amount and nature of light to which they are exposed. A strip lamp is built into the scanning head too, providing a bright, calibrated light source that shines up at your face-down photo on the glass plate and reflects back down through a lens onto the CCDs.

Flatbed scanners, therefore, capture images one narrow strip at a time across the width of the CCD array. The scanning head moves down an increment, another strip is captured, and so on. For this reason, flatbed scanners are usually given a dual resolution specification such as 600x1200dpi or 1200x2400dpi. The lower figure in the pair is the actual optical sampling rate of the CCD array across the width of the plate, while the higher

3
An economical flatbed scanner is sufficient for most Web imaging needs. Look for a sturdily built model with at least 24-bit color and a slide adaptor.

4
Good scanning software will not only let you operate the device, but will provide color correction tools such as highlight-shadow histograms.

5
You may be given tone correction curves, which let you enhance an image in ways that contrast and brightness controls alone could never achieve.

1
The basic workings of a flatbed scanner couldn't be simpler: a scanning head and lamp pass under the glass plate, and the reflected light from the photo sitting on the glass is sent back via mirrors to the lens and CCD arrangement.

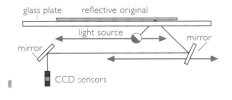

2
A transparency adaptor in most flatbed scanners is nothing more than a second lamp unit, putting the light source above the photo and shining through to the scanning head below.

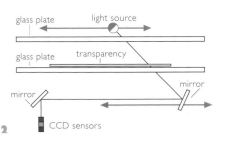

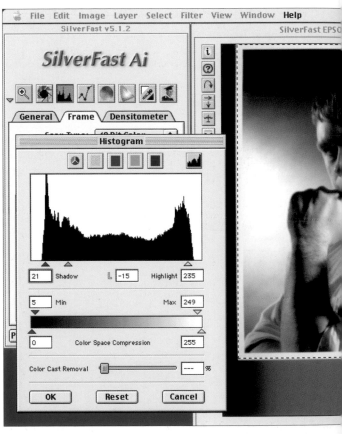

20

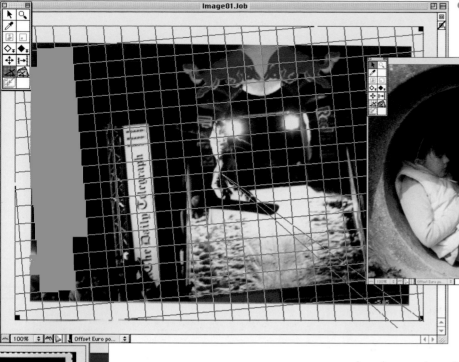

6

Having a set of controls for altering the hues within an image while you scan is increasingly common. This avoids wasting time in a photo-editing program afterward.

7

Some of the better scanning software programs include special features to make the scanning process itself easier, such as this tilt adjustment tool in Linocolor Elite.

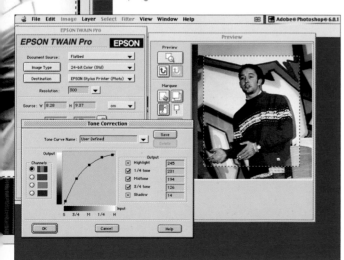

figure indicates the increment at which the scanning head can physically move from one end of the plate to the other. These scanners are called "flatbed," by the way, primarily to distinguish them from prepress drum scanners, which spin images on a cylinder, and from film scanners, which move photo transparencies in a special holder across a fixed scanning head.

Because Web images themselves do not boast a high resolution, it's not necessary to insist on high "dpi" figures in the specification. The exception is when you need to blow up small originals, such as cropped pictures and transparencies. It's also possible to upgrade many cheap scanners with so-called transparency adaptors, while many mid-priced products come with such adaptors already provided. A conventional transparency adaptor is simply a replacement lid containing a second lamp that passes above (effectively behind) any transparency on the glass plate, shining the light through to the scanning head below. Certain more expensive flatbed scanners incorporate transparency scanning inside the unit, film-scanner style (see page 26).

5

MAKING YOUR FIRST SCAN

It's all too easy to be suckered into the simplicity of flatbed scanning and assume that obtaining a decent image capture is virtually automatic. No wonder so many images end up being rescanned over and over again until the desired result is achieved. Whether you're new to scanning or are finding the whole task a bit too hit-and-miss for your liking, follow our six-step guide to getting it right the first time.

Step 1: Get a preview

Let's assume you want to capture a standard reflective original such as a photo. Lift the lid of the scanner and place your photo face down onto the glass. Run the scanning software, which is often available as a TWAIN-compatible driver or Photoshop-compatible plug-in and accessed from the File menu. Locate the Prescan or Preview button in the software interface and click on it. The scanner will pop into life and present you with a quick, refreshed preview image of what's on the scanning plate.

Step 2: Crop your image tightly

Every scanning software provides a marquee selection tool for designating a rectangular area over the preview that you would like to be scanned properly. But don't scan yet—you've only just started. Make sure the crop you drag out is as tight as possible to the image area you really want, and especially make sure you haven't included any frame borders. Over-large crops prolong scanning times, and extraneous image information will adversely affect subsequent color enhancement.

Step 3: Pinch the histogram

Resist the temptation to click on any auto-exposure or auto-correct button in the software; if it has already happened, look for a way of undoing the changes or

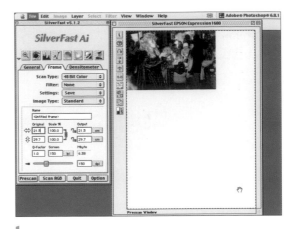

1

2

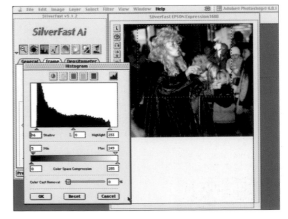

3

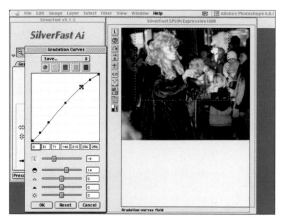

4

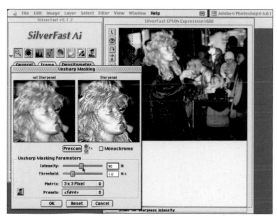

5

6

switching them off. Then if the scanning software provides a histogram control, use it to pinch the highlight and shadow extremes (usually presented as white and black triangle sliders) inward to meet the edges of the histogram itself. This removes the flatness in an image and improves contrast without affecting color tones.

Step 4: Nudge the curve

If the scanning software also provides a tonal or gradation curve control, use it. But do so with caution. Initially, the curve should be a straight diagonal line. Tugging it into a great bowed curve will destroy the image with a gaudy 1970s psychedelic effect. Usually the best results come from nudging the line into a very gentle—barely perceptible even—S-wave.

Step 5: Sharpen the image capture

All image captures should be sharpened at the point of scanning rather than afterward in your photo-editing software. This will ensure that you lose the minimum image information in the process. Where possible, use "unsharp masking" in preference to a plain "sharpen" filter. This plain sharpen filter is somewhat indiscriminate about what, and how, it sharpens. The unsharp mask method, by contrast, offers more control and can be configured to not to sharpen any unwanted elements.

Step 6: Resize and scan your image

Forget scan resolutions and dpi. Instead, enter the physical size that you want the scanned image to be. In Web imaging, you should set this size in pixels, not millimeters or points. Resizing now during scanning rather than afterward in software will avoid image information being lost. When you're ready, click the Scan button.

23

DIGITAL STILL CAMERAS AND STORAGE MEDIA

Flatbed scanners are fine for capturing photographs you already have, but are an unnecessary intermediate hassle if you intend to capture fresh pictures specifically taken for the job. Instead of shooting film, developing, printing, and scanning, go straight from shutter-snap to computer screen with a digital camera.

To be precise, we're talking about digital "still" cameras as opposed to digital video devices as mentioned on page 27. That said, there are strong similarities between the two types of product in terms of core technology. Digital cameras feature a rectangular area CCD array as opposed to a scanner's striplike linear array: this is the digital "film" behind the lens that captures the image. However, unlike a conventional film camera, most digital cameras don't actually have a shutter at all. Instead, the image seen by the CCD array is fed to a small color LCD (liquid crystal display) screen on the back of the camera in real time, just as it is in a camcorder. It's only when you press the so-called shutter button that the frame is captured and saved.

Obviously the great benefit of a digital camera for Web designers is that you can transfer the digital images to your computer immediately. Many time-sensitive Web sites, such as news services and sports publishers, prefer digital cameras to conventional cameras for this very reason.

Digital cameras are still very expensive compared with their film counterparts, but prices are falling as fast as quality and resolution are increasing. Although digital cameras are usually rated according to their CCD density, measured as the number of pixels rounded to the nearest million (2 megapixels, 3 megapixels, and so on), the big price jumps come when a camera supports better lenses, includes more file storage, and so on. At the other extreme, the cheapest models won't even have an LCD window for previewing your shots.

When choosing a digital camera at any level, look for product features such as long battery life and removable storage. For maximum versatility, you may also want the camera to provide a hot shoe for standard flash

1
Cheap, entry-level, digital cameras such as the Epson 2100 have only the most basic features, but image quality will be sufficient for most Web display needs.

2
Trade up to a mid-range camera such as the FujiFilm 2800Z and you can expect to get more memory, the capacity to preview images and better image quality.

3
Top-quality digital cameras such as the Canon EOS D30 do not come cheap. But they are fast becoming an essential tool for professional photographers.

attachments, a tripod thread, manual focus override, and maybe even support for exchangeable zoom and wide-angle lenses. Many Web designers also find a "macro mode" useful for shooting objects close-up, not least for e-commerce applications. Expert photographers will also want manual exposure controls and white point compensation for artificial light environments.

Some digital still cameras can record audio and short video clips too, just as some digital camcorders can capture stills. These may not have obvious uses for Web design, but it's worth considering their potential.

Digital cameras behave in almost exactly the same way as film cameras—except that the image is recorded onto digital recording media instead of film. Usually this media is removable and behaves just like a floppy or hard drive, except with no moving parts (with the exception of the IBM Microdrive).

Currently, the two most popular types of digital camera memory are ultra-thin 1¾ x 1½ x 1/16 in SmartMedia (SM) cards and the slightly thicker (1½ x 1¾ x 2/16 in)

CompactFlash (CF) cards. The former are currently available in capacities up to 128Mb, while CompactFlash cards can now be purchased in capacities up to 512Mb—that's capacity enough to store 80 uncompressed 3.34Mb photos, 433 low compression JPEG files, and about 1,700 images in economy mode! If you can afford the higher-capacity cards, you can keep on shooting for a long time before there's any need to make more room on the card.

SmartMedia and CompactFlash cards are manufactured by a variety of companies so the pricing is competitive (though never cheap enough!). For high-demand photographers there's also the large capacity IBM Microdrive. This is actually a miniature hard drive that comes in 340Mb, 500Mb, and 1Gb capacities and fits neatly into the camera's CompactFlash card slot.

You can download the images directly off a memory card using its universal serial bus cable or via a third-party card reader. The latter option involves the expense of yet another accessory, but is a quicker method.

25

6
Nixvue Digital Album weighs in at only 11 ounces. This portable storage device is designed specifically for digital photography, and will download the contents of CompactFlash, SmartMedia, and Memory Stick removable memory cards onto its internal 2.5-inch 10-gigabyte hard drive.

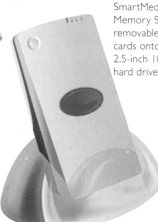

4
Currently there is a choice of four types of image recording media: CompactFlash, SmartMedia, Memory Stick, and SD card. The first two are widely accepted by a range of products whereas Sony's Memory Stick and Panasonic's SD card are only compatible with those branded products.

5
Because of the variety of card memory formats, some manufacturers have designed multicard readers: the Multitech drive here reads both SmartMedia and CompactFlash cards in one unit, but using separate slots.

ADVANCED SCANNERS AND CAMERAS

Earlier we pointed out that it's not necessary to pay large sums of money for high-end imaging equipment, simply because the Web is essentially a low-resolution medium. But there are exceptions. When the quality of your imagery is essential, not least when dealing with corporate clients and e-commerce sites where nothing less than the best will do, it's worth looking at advanced image-capture products.

Also, don't be suckered too far into the concept of low resolution. More important is the relative physical size of the onscreen images on different computers. So while a 50-pixel-wide picture will look pretty chunky on a 640x480 pixel notebook screen, it'll be pretty insignificant on a 21-inch monitor running at 1600x1200 pixels. A Web site for a photographer's portfolio or a digital picture library, for example, will need larger and therefore better-quality images.

A professional photographer, or even a keen amateur, should consider buying a film scanner. This device uses the same technology as a flatbed scanner but is designed solely for capturing transparencies and negatives at a very high resolution, from 2,400dpi upward, and at vastly superior quality. Models are available that accommodate a wide range of professional film sizes, including 9x6cm. Entry-level film scanners tend only to support 35mm shots, and sometimes Advanced Photo Sytem (APS) reels too.

26

3

1

2

3
Modern digital video editing packages such as Adobe Premiere have taken a tip from the entry-level programs and introduced drag-and-drop storyboard editing for easy assembly of clips.

4
Don't forget that in order for a video to be complete, it needs a soundtrack. Working on smooth audio transitions from clip to clip is an important—and often time-consuming—task.

1
The Agfa DuoScan T1200 is well suited for capturing images for use on the Web with both a flatbed for reflective art work and a separate tray for scanning slide materials.

2
A Nikon Coolscan IV dedicated film scanner, ideal for 35mm and APS formats.

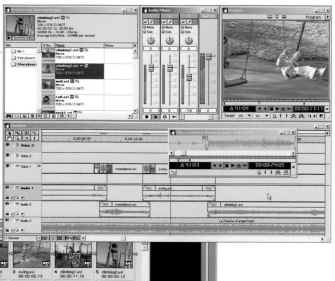

Film scanners are good for dealing with a backlog of old transparencies, but the forward-looking photographer might want to invest in a high-quality digital still camera. Remember, the ultimate determining factor in digital camera quality is the same as for conventional film cameras: the lenses. On the other hand, you may wish to save the money destined for cameras and film scanners, then spend it on a flatbed scanner capable of capturing poster-sized originals. Though it's not a very exciting solution in a digital age, it's possibly the most versatile one for the day-to-day designer.

Of course, still images are just the start. Cutting-edge Web design often involves animation and video, so you might want to dive in with a digital video (DV) camcorder.

Both Mac OS X and Windows XP include DV editing utilities for free, but they're not enough for Web imaging. It's not just the editing, but the final format, that matters. You will need a professional-class editing package that can export to a highly compressed "streamable" video file. Streaming allows a movie to play on a Web site visitor's computer without the whole thing having to be downloaded first, and is therefore essential if you don't want to put visitors off.

5
After the edit, you will need to process the video sequence to a compressed, streamable format for putting on the Web. Here, Cleaner EZ reports speed and size as it encodes the movie on a frame-by-frame basis.

6
Like most things digital, digital video cameras are getting better and more affordable.

7
A top-quality digital camera is not required for most Web imaging needs but is fast becoming an essential tool for professional photographers.

PICTURE LIBRARIES

Every good designer knows when to supplement scans and self-shot photos with stock images from a picture library. Stock images and clip art can fill the gaps when you need something fast, and can save you a lot of time, money, and effort for "cover" shots and branding imagery.

Most graphics software these days comes supplied with a heap of clip media, ranging from cartoon graphics to tiling textures, patterns, and digital photos. To be honest, most of this free stuff tends to be rather cheesy and clichéd, and often the photos have been scanned poorly. But you can occasionally find some gems in there if you care to look. Especially useful these days are ready-made Web buttons that come complete with JavaScript rollover states, page backgrounds, icon graphics, and animated GIFs. Just remember to evaluate them with a cynical designer's eye rather than that of a Web enthusiast.

1
The royalty-free "Executive People" collection from PhotoEssentials makes a fresh change from clichéd images of people shaking hands and banknotes.

2
People working out at the gym is still a popular subject, but setting up these shots yourself would be a nightmare. Luckily, royalty-free libraries on CD make it easy.

3
Some stock photo categories can be broadly thematic. "Busy People" is a collection of all kinds of people doing different things, but they all seem … well, busy.

4
This CD-based collection is another with a broadly cross-topic theme: "Modern Living." This way, you are more likely to get extended usage from the one library, due to lack of duplication.

5
Many photo publishers are now represented under the Getty Images banner, including longtime favorite PhotoDisc. This means you can browse a number of collections at one site.

6
EyeWire sells clip media on CD-ROM but also offers the best of its library for online browsing and individual download. Photo libraries are in the enviable position of being able to use their own pictures on their Web site.

7
Online browsing can reveal shots you hadn't expected, such as the kiteboarding snaps here at the Stone site, found when searching for surfing pictures.

For professional-class stock images, you should approach a picture library. These days, practically all picture libraries are fully digitized, so you don't even need to do any scanning. Better still, they are all accessible over the Internet 24 hours a day.

In addition to this pay-per-use method, the market for royalty-free stock images has been growing enormously over recent years. Royalty free means you only pay once, after which you're free to reuse the image as you wish, within reason. You can purchase images at certain online libraries on a royalty-free basis, but much better value can be obtained by buying stock CDs. This way you get a whole CD full of images on a similar theme, usually for the price of just a few shots bought individually; besides, a CD is much faster to browse through than a graphics-filled library Web site.

The only big drawback with stock photos is that you don't at any time own the images or have any exclusivity rights over them. Having chosen a picture for your Web site, if you subsequently discover someone else has used the same image for theirs, that's just tough luck.

29

LOOKING AT BIT DEPTH

Bit depth is the amount of "bits" or "binary digits" used to define a specific tone or range of tones. The higher the bit depth, the more detail is contained in an image. One-bit, for example, will produce only black and white (the bit is either on or off), whereas an 8-bit image will generate 256 grays or colors (256 is the maximum number of permutations of a string of eight 1s and 0s). Most color scanners and digital cameras produce images that are 24-bit color (three times 8-bit, "R", "G," and "B"). Anything over 24-bit is "supersampled" to a higher level, commonly 36-bit, 42-bit, and even 48-bit color.

A 48-bit scan from a color original will produce a file approximately twice the size of a 24-bit scan (8Mb as opposed to 16Mb). A 36- or 48-bit scanner will capture more detail in the highlighted and shadowed areas of an image than a 24-bit scanner might, so you must consider the amount of detail needed in any image you use. Even when a 36-bit scan is converted to conventional 24-bit afterward for editing, its tonal range will be better than if you had captured it at 24-bit to start with.

Because bit depth has an influence on image quality, it is a factor to keep in mind when manipulating images and creating an image archive. Although most image-manipulation and Web-building software programs only work in 24-bit color, you will always benefit from starting out with a larger bit-depth original even if it has to be converted or downsampled to a smaller bit depth for editing at a later stage. For this reason it is always a good idea to include any raw or high bit-depth files in a master file in case you want to perform some advanced editing on the same image at a later date.

1 | 2
While 1-bit defines a simple black-and-white image, 2-bit allocates an additional two colors or grays in between. Digital "grayscale" pictures are normally 8-bit images with 254 levels of gray plus black and white.

3 | 4
High bit-depth images (more than 8-bit) will always produce better-quality images— even if the files are subsequently reduced to 8-bit for editing, printing, or displaying on the Web. Though the 8-bit color scan (above) appears slightly brighter and richer in color, the 16-bit version (right) has a slight edge in the shadow detail.

4

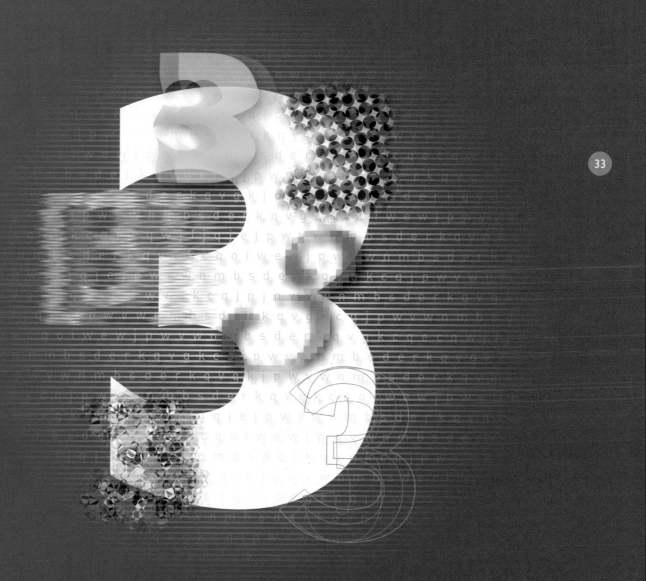

CORE IMAGING SOFTWARE

Everyone involved in Web design needs image-manipulation software. Obviously it's the focus of this book, but even the most technical of HTML authors will need some graphics to shape up their content. It's not enough to own Web site creation software or a graphics package; whether you're a Web author or dedicated designer, you need both.

In the first instance, you need the imaging software to handle the pictures you have captured with scanners and digital cameras, or obtained from stock photo libraries and clip media collections. This software can be used as a simple color correction device or to execute the most complex of image changes, all from within the same program.

Besides, pictures need to be cropped, resized, and reformatted for use on the Web. Although these are basic features supported by most graphics packages on the market, including the very cheap consumer products, professional image manipulation software can be used to create entirely new artwork or to combine sourced images (Web graphics, photographs, and vector art) into multilayered, many-faceted images.

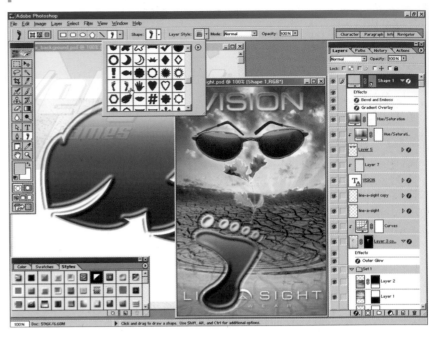

1

1
The standard imaging application for design professionals is Adobe Photoshop. No other package offers such a versatile range of manipulation tools for print and Web graphics.

2
Adobe has also developed a simplified version of Photoshop, which it calls Photoshop Elements. This is targeted at the home user and photography enthusiast, and is provided with many user-friendly automated functions.

3
MGI PhotoSuite is one of the most popular photo-editing packages around, thanks to widespread bundling with digital cameras. It is very good for basic image enhancement and can even handle some advanced Web graphic features.

2

3

34

6

Micrografx Picture Publisher enjoys a loyal user base even among professionals, despite the dominance of Photoshop. The latest release supports many Web-specific features such as slicing.

7

Unique among mainstream imaging software, Deneba Canvas mixes vector and bitmap editing in one program. It's a very powerful photo-enhancement and manipulation package for Web users, if a rather unconventional one.

4

Corel's answer to Photoshop is Photo-Paint. It's not a direct copy of Adobe's market leader, but is arguably as powerful for most image-manipulation tasks, and includes several clever real-media brushes. Photo-Paint is part of the Corel Graphics Suite along with the vector graphics program CorelDraw.

5

Arguably the world's favorite general-purpose imaging software for the PC, Jasc's Paint Shop Pro is geared toward practical bitmap editing, enhancement, and composition. It also supports vector graphics and comes with a GIF animation utility.

Core image-manipulation software can be loosely categorized into three groups:
• basic consumer programs—these are generally project-based, cost less than $70 and have limited functions.
• semiprofessional programs costing between $70 and $200, being packed with a wide range of features from print to Web, and often targeted at serious digital photographers.
• professional applications costing in excess of $400, suited for all onscreen RGB and print CMYK tasks.

Although our focus in this book is on the professional level, don't discount some of those semiprofessional software packages. They are often built with very strong Web-related features and automated routines, which can make life easier compared with doing everything manually in a high-end package. Remember the adage: biggest is best, but not always for you.

SPECIALIST IMAGING SOFTWARE

Image manipulation might be your core graphics application in Web design, but it's far from being the only one. Depending upon the kind of imagery you want to use on your sites, you may need something a little more specialist. These will be imaging packages that add to your overall toolkit rather than supplant the core software.

Most commonly, a designer will want to reproduce real-media artwork: that is, pictures created the conventional way with oils, watercolors, chalks, crayons, and pencils. As well as producing an attractive impressionist, textured feel to some of your graphic ideas, real-media artwork is an effective antidote to the overbearing "tech" feel of the Web in general. Paintings and drawings are warmer and more human than so many reprocessed photos and sterile Web buttons.

Certain photo-editing packages provide paint tools that emulate the visual effect of real-media brushes. But other specialist software exists that can handle the task much better, more accurately, and more realistically. A particular application of real-media painting in software

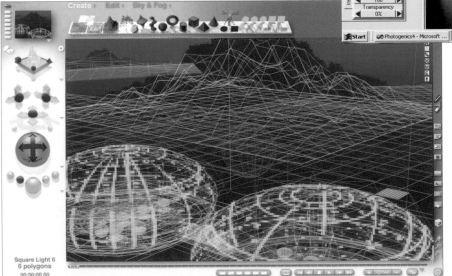

1
Procreate Painter is the classic real-media effect imaging package, letting you paint and draw with tools which really do look like conventional oils, watercolours, pastels and so on.

3
Corel Bryce is 3D made simple enough for everyone, but it is still a specialist application within its field. You'd use Bryce for creating photo-realistic landscapes and scenes, which can turn out to be first-rate image maps for a stylish site.

2
Idruna Photogenics is sold as a photo-editing tool, but it's completely unlike any other on the market. The program frees your mind with the ability to tweak, swirl, and paint through multiple image layers in a highly interactive fashion.

is "rotoscoping," the process of drawing on each frame of a movie. This can be done with digital videos in software now, but only using specialist packages.

It may also be the case that you want to produce expressive digital graphics that go beyond the conventional, but your core imaging software doesn't come with enough filter effects. You can invest in third-party plug-ins, of course, or look around for unconventional software products that manipulate images in ways you may never have thought possible.

You will at some point want to consider using some 3D graphics software. Although the world of 3D is a grand topic in itself, not to mention hugely complex, there are many software programs on the market that are targeted at general designers, and increasingly Web designers. Unless you want to go into 3D in a big way, you are only likely to want to create 3D effect textures and scenes, shaded objects, navigational elements, and maybe even posed characters. All these tasks are possible in user-friendly packages without the need for architectural training or an engineering degree simply to understand the terminology.

37

4
Fancy generating your own Web site virtual presenter along the lines of Ananova? Try Curious Labs' Poser, a compelling package that lets you manipulate digital mannequins, built with mix-and-match body parts.

5
Synthetix Studio Artist provides a number of Painter-like real-media tools, using a photo under the paint layer to act as digital paint for your brush strokes over the top. Studio Artist is also designed for digital video rotoscoping.

6
If you want to develop unique character models that look convincing, but again without having to know 3D design inside-out, Pixologic's ZBrush might be the answer. As you can see, the results can be outstandingly effective.

OPTIMIZATION SOFTWARE

Good Web images must do more than look good and be in the right file format. Since the vast majority of Web users access the Internet through relatively slow dial-up modem services, the files themselves need to be as small as possible so that they download as quickly as possible. At best, achieving the right balance between size and quality can be a time-consuming task of trial and error; at worst, it's a matter of potluck.

Thankfully, professional image-manipulation software comes with facilities to evaluate size and quality visually. It's a function known as optimization, and usually kicks in when you save or export an image to one of the Web-standard formats, namely JPEG, GIF, or PNG. The most basic approach is to present you with a twin-pane preview window: one shows the original image you're working on, and the other previews how it will look when saved in the appropriate Web file format. This allows you to experiment with the compression level in a JPEG, for example, or the number of colors in a GIF.

Some Web optimizing software will present additional information that the Web designer will find useful. Most commonly, you will see the compressed file size as a figure measured in bytes, along with an

38

2
Spot the difference: Adobe ImageReady employs pretty much the same approach as Fireworks. But while Photoshop uses a similar system when exporting to Web formats, here in ImageReady it's part of the working interface.

3
Most general-use image manipulation software provides Web optimization functions, again with before-and-after preview panes and image controls, as shown here in Corel Photo-Paint. Such features take the guesswork out of balancing image quality and file size.

1
Macromedia Fireworks presents the now-classic multipane interface for Web optimization, showing the original image alongside a Web-format version, together with optimization options in a palette.

1

3

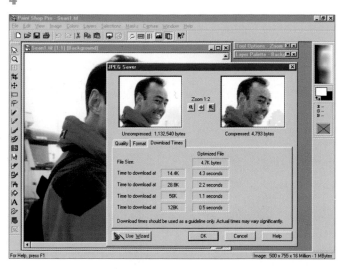

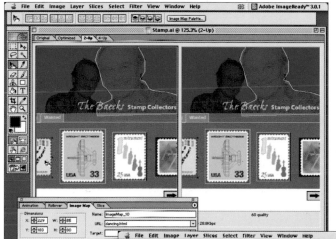

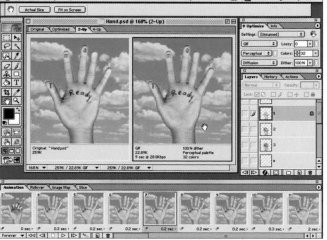

indication of how many seconds it will take for that file to be downloaded across a particular class of modem. This lets you make informed choices about image quality by targeting your designs at a particular audience. For example, while it may be common to evaluate download speeds for a 28.8K modem, most Western consumers with disposable incomes own 56K modems. Similarly, large businesses typically access the Web across broadband network connections of 576K or faster.

Certain image-processing software packages are custom-made for optimizing Web graphics, and these have obvious advantages. They will also generate image maps, HTML slices, rollovers, and maybe animations. Just be warned that cheaper programs only offer a simple export filter: they will convert images to the right format and may even do a good job of the compression-quality ratio, but you'll have no control over how it's applied.

4 Optimization filters are available in many cheaper, mid-range packages too, such as Paint Shop Pro. Note the download time estimates for different modem speeds.

5 Specialist Web graphics software such as ImageReady provides image-mapping tools, although increasingly you will find these in general graphics programs too, and even certain desktop publishing applications.

6 One function that dedicated Web optimization programs can boast over general-use packages is the ability to build, process, and save GIF animations, with the help of a multiframe timeline.

39

VECTOR IMAGING SOFTWARE

Vector-based imagery is made up of mathematical definitions of the picture parts. In contrast, a bitmap image is constructed with a matrix of pixels. For example, a vector file of a line would record the start and end points, thickness, type, and color of the line. A bitmap version would record the brightness and color of each pixel that not only made up the line but also all the white space that surrounded it. As the vector file contains less information, it is smaller than its bitmap counterpart. Bitmap images are great for photographic pictures as they can record the gradual tonal changes of an objects surface, whereas vector is more suited to displaying flat colored, regularly shaped, graphic objects.

The one distinct advantage vector files have over bitmap is that they are infinitely scaleable. Vector images can be rescaled or resized with no loss of quality, whereas we all know that any bitmap digital camera image or scanned file has a finite enlargability. Blow them up too big and you'll see artifacts, fuzziness, and other unpleasant image problems. Because of this

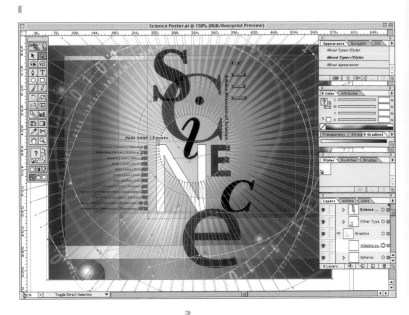

1

The vector tools of Illustrator are similar to the pen tools of Photoshop, and paths created in one can be used in the other.

2 | 3

CorelDraw is an excellent graphics tool with a large band of devotees. It is normally available as part of a graphics suite that includes the highly regarded Photo-Paint and R.A.V.E, a Web animations package.

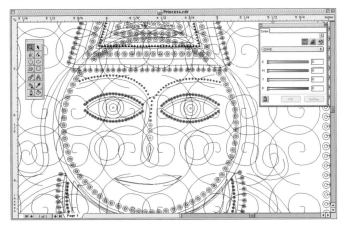

CorelDraw vector view

CorelDraw illustration view

40

infinite expandability, vector graphics can be quickly scaled to print resolutions and higher, should a client require. Photoshop (version six and above) includes vector-based text facilities. This has brought an unheard-of creative freedom to the world's favorite bitmap-based image-editing program.

So, how does vector image-creation software improve digital imaging?

In a nutshell, 2D and 3D graphic illustrations with infinite scaleability can be created using a range of easy-to-use graphics, painting, transparency, and perspective tools. The two largest players, Adobe and Macromedia, have streamlined their products to include an interface and toolset similar to those in their respective bitmap editing programs so that it's easier to jump from one program to the other without going through a steep learning curve.

Vector graphics are superior to bitmap images not only for their editability but also for their suitability in creating high-quality tone gradients, accurate drawing tools, and economically-sized Web animations—as well as their ability to export Macromedia Flash files and other interactive file material.

Currently the best vector-based image creation software packages include Adobe Illustrator, CorelDraw, and Macromedia FreeHand.

The bottom line is that most of the things you can do with vector programs can be executed almost instantly—not after watching the egg timer crawl across your screen for ten minutes.

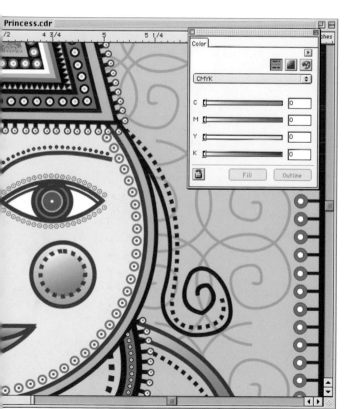

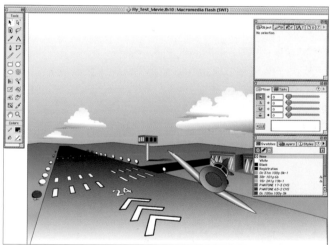

4
Macromedia's FreeHand is a very advanced product that goes beyond purely illustrative tools to provide substantial Web graphics features including, as shown here, the ability to create and test Flash animations.

FILE FORMATS I

When an image is created by a digital camera or desktop scanner, you'll need to save the information created as a computer data file. Digital cameras save the data onto the camera's removable floppy disk, from which it can be transferred to a computer for manipulation. If the image is from a scanner, you'll have several choices about which format to choose, either through the scanner driver software or the imaging software proper.

As there are up to fifteen different file formats in most photo-editing programs, to avoid wasting time and resources it's important to have a basic understanding of which are most suited for imaging and Web applications.

Image file formats can be divided into two classes: those that preserve all the original photo data and those that, in an effort to make the file smaller, discard information in the saving process. The first is termed a lossless file and the second is a lossy file.

JPEG (Joint Photographic Experts Group)

JPEG files feature a variable compression algorithm that permits you to select the file size (and therefore the degree of image degradation experienced) before it is saved to disk. For example, though a typical three-megapixel digital camera might store only one single lossless TIFF image on a removable 16Mb SmartMedia card, you might be able to cram more than 200 JPEG files onto the same card, with only a minimum loss of quality (depending on how much compression is set).

The higher the compression value set for a JPEG file, the smaller the file size, and the greater the quality loss experienced. If the compression is set to the lowest ratio, say 1:2.7, a JPEG file might be indistinguishable from the same file saved in a lossless format.

For almost every image application, low-compression JPEG files provide just the right balance between quality and available storage space.

1
Vector graphic as GIF: there are only 19 different colors in this image, so GIF compression easily shrank it down to 8.4Kb.

2
Photo image as GIF: the GIF format needs all 256 index colors to reproduce continuous-tone photos, hence the 72Kb file size.

Because JPEG files can be reduced to minuscule file sizes, this is an ideal format for transmitting over the Internet—a 3.5Mb file can be compressed to anything from 688 kilobytes (at the "best" setting) to a file as tiny as 60 kilobytes (at the "smallest" compression setting). That's the difference between 228 seconds and 16 seconds for an image to be sent over the Internet using a 28.8Kbps modem. You could probably reduce these file sizes even more using a specialist image-compression software such as Mr Sid or BitJazz. The only disadvantage of using one of these third-party products is that you'll need to buy the software to open the file.

Note that if the JPEG file is opened and saved repeatedly, the image quality will progressively worsen. It's better to open a JPEG file once and then save it in a lossless format, such as a TIFF file, to stop progressive degradation.

3
Vector graphic as JPEG: since JPEG can't take advantage of indexed or palettized colors, the best it could achieve here was 30Kb.

5
Vector graphic as PNG: this format has the benefit of being able to compress neatly in both indexed and 24-bit color modes, and achieves 10Kb here.

4
Photo image as JPEG: without any effort, this photo was saved to a 21Kb file, which is less than one-third of the size of the GIF version.

4

6
Photo image as PNG: some additional optimization work might be necessary, but standard PNG format compresses the photo to under 60Kb.

6

TIFF (Tagged Image File Format)

TIFF files can be saved uncompressed or compressed at without suffering image degradation using an algorithm called LZW. Compressed files take longer to open than uncompressed files. TIFF files can be saved in either PC or Mac byte orders. Whether or not PCs can read Mac TIFF files depends on the imaging software being used; Macs can read both. TIFF files undoubtedly give the best results for print, in terms of sharpness and clarity, and are good for storing your "master files," but JPEG files are the only files to use for photographic images on the Web.

GIF (Graphics Interchange Format)

As the name suggests, GIF is best used for transmitting and saving graphics on the Web. GIFs only operate in Indexed Color mode. This means that their color range is limited to 256 colors or less. The colors in the original image are indexed (approximated) to the smaller range available in the GIF format. If your photo editor has a "Save for Web" feature, you might be able to optimize a GIF further by using this feature to reduce the number of colors in the file's palette—a powerful feature if you are working primarily on the Web.

PNG (Portable Network Graphics)

PNG is a comparatively new format for the Internet. PNG images look similar to JPEG files, but have the advantages of improved quality, higher bit depth, better compression technology, and the ability to import Alpha channels that allow you to preserve transparency. However, only use this format if you don't mind losing a part of your potential audience as it is only supported by more recent browsers.

FILE FORMATS 2

1
TIFF and EPS formats can contain extra information for producing cut-out images, that is those with the background removed. One system is to trace around the object carefully and save it as a path.

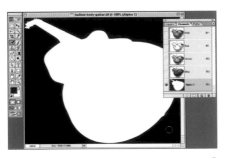

2
Another approach is to paint a mask over the unwanted background area using brush tools, saving it as an alpha channel. Again, most layout packages use the embedded alpha channel to generate a cut-out path.

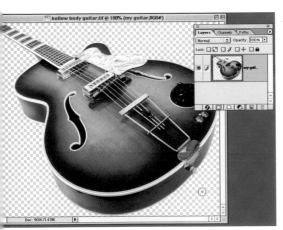

3
Alternatively, use Photoshop to delete the unwanted areas of the image, leaving them transparent. The file can then be saved in Photoshop's native PSD format, which is supported by many layout programs.

RAW (Raw data)

The RAW file format is a proprietary format used by Canon and Kodak, among others, for storing high bit-depth images before bringing them into smaller bit-depth photo manipulation programs, such as Adobe Photoshop. Once converted to a TIFF or JPEG there's little advantage in resaving in the RAW format.

EPS (Encapsulated PostScript)

EPS files, like JPEG, can be read on both PCs and Macs. They are particularly suited for use with images or graphics destined for PostScript printing devices. Layout programs such as QuarkXPress, Adobe InDesign, and Adobe Pagemaker all support the EPS file format, as do Adobe Photoshop and many others. Files can be saved with ASCII, Binary, or JPEG encoding, depending on the platform, and can include other information such as a halftone screen and color-management profile. Stick with the TIFF or JPEG format if the file is a photographic one.

PSD

This Photoshop-specific file format is the format of choice if you want to preserve Photoshop's layers, as well as its Paths and Alpha Channels. However, saving layers does add considerably to the final file size.

PDF (Portable Document Format)

Adobe Portable Document Format files are incredibly versatile. Using Adobe's Acrobat Distiller, you can create files from any kind of publishing document. Acrobat Reader, the mini program used to open and display PDF files, is available free online. PDFs are ideal for transmitting entire documents over the Internet. You can even use them to notate and edit documents, articles, and books before returning them to the publisher or prepress house for changes and final checking.

JPEG 2000

The emerging JPEG 2000 format is not a replacement for JPEG, but an expanded still-image file format. The idea is to bring together various technologies into a single standard. It incorporates wavelet technology for extreme compression and maintains multiple image resolutions across layers. This means a single JPEG 2000 image could support Web-page quality and high-end press quality without rescanning or other special treatment. Although the standard has yet to be supported by major graphics applications, it is likely to be of interest to cross-media publishers who want to repurpose print and Web content automatically through XML.

Other file formats and compression terms

Photoshop's DCS (Desktop Color Separation) A version of the EPS format that enables color separations to be created. Each DCS file holds five separate files: four (CMYK) color channels and a preview file.

FlashPix A file format (created jointly by Kodak and Live Picture) based on the latter's IVUE pyramid file structure. When you open a FlashPix image, only the information for that magnification is displayed. Zoom in and another resolution is created. Bitmapped images display *all* their information on screen at the same time, so are more cumbersome to handle.

LZW Compression (Lemple-Zif-Welch) The primary lossless compression for the TIFF file format. Slow to save and open, LZW compression is supported by GIF, TIFF, PDF, and PostScript languages.

Run Length Encoding (RLE) A lossless compression technique supported by Photoshop and some Windows file formats.

ZIP Encoding A lossless compression technique supported by PDF and TIFF file formats. Effective with files with large areas of single color.

5
GIF supports a transparency matte, so cut-outs are possible, allowing the Web page background to show through. But it's an on-off matte, leaving the edges jaggy.

4
Cut-outs are supported by Web image file formats too, but not all of them and not all in the same way. No matter which of the previous methods you try, a JPEG will always fill the background with a solid color, white by default.

45

6
PNG can contain full alpha channel transparency, including gradient masks and anti-aliased edges. This produces a better quality cut-out. Unfortunately, not all Web browsers support PNG.

THE INSTANT IMAGE FIX

All of us, almost without exception, go for the instant image fix-up—the automated one-mouse-click solution. It's faster, simpler, and nine times out of ten, works the way we want it to. Such fixes include automatically improving the color, contrast, saturation, and sharpness of images, bumping up the quality of raw scanned files, improving the quality of imported video footage, and even improving overly compressed JPEG downloads from the Web. For those times where the one-button solution doesn't work, we have to resort to using techniques that offer more specific image control. We'll deal with those later in this section.

Usually the best programs for instant fixes are the midrange photo manipulation products—the ones targeted at digital photographers. These are the most likely to come with automatic one-click correction functions for color, lighting, and exposure, plus custom tools for removing scratches and unwanted effects such as red-eye. Professional image manipulation software can do all this too, of course, but there are fewer automated routines—it's all rather more hands-on in approach.

1
There's something wrong with this original photo, but what is it that needs fixing? Is the film fogged or the image poorly scanned? Does it lack color or contrast or shadow? Call in the instant fix!

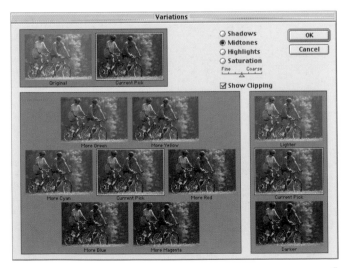

2
Here's the result of running the Auto Levels command found in most photo manipulation programs, including Photoshop.

3
A similar result was achieved with the Auto Contrast command, although close inspection reveals tiny differences in color.

4
Alternatively, experiment with contrast, levels, and hues simultaneously using the Variations approach, offered by Photoshop, and other packages. Just click on the preferred image to apply the effects.

48

5 | 6

You have to look twice at this picture to realize that there's anything of interest in it, namely London's Big Ben clock tower. The reason is that the colors are flat and gray, so nothing stands out. This can be fixed quickly if you don't know what to do manually. Here we've called up Paint Shop Pro's Automatic Saturation Enhancement effect. All we have to do is choose a "bias" (whether to saturate the colors more or less) and an overall strength.

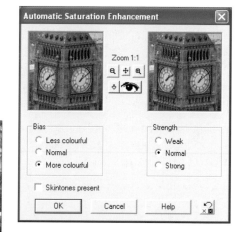

7

The result is more than just a slightly more colorful image. Increasing the saturation reveals a brown tinge to the entire Palace of Westminster, helping it stand out from the mass of nondescript buildings behind.

8 | 9

Most instant fixes are solutions for the casual photographer. Take this point-and-shoot camera snap, where the flash has produced a red-eye effect. The Red-eye Removal palette in Paint Shop Pro lets you draw a circle over the offending red area and choose an iris color, then the program does the rest for you.

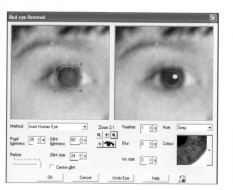

10

The result, though imprecise by professional standards, is an astonishing transformation all the same. It may have been just an instant fix, but it has created an acceptable amateur shot out of a totally unusable one.

49

CONTROLLING TONE USING LEVELS

In Photoshop open an image and select the Levels command (Alt/Command "L" or Image>Adjust>Levels, from the dropdown menu). Quite often images sourced directly from digital cameras or scanners display a flat contrast—this can be fixed using the Levels feature.

The Levels dialog box displays all the tones in a picture as a graph. This is called a histogram, or tone graph. The shadow values are to the left and highlight values are displayed to the right. Try clicking the "Auto" tab in the dialog box. This usually does the trick of adjusting the contrast level or adding a color change to compensate for a color cast, if it is needed. Because this is an auto setting it might not go far enough, or it might go too far for your purposes.

A more accurate method of adjusting the tonal range is to manually click and drag the triangular end points located at the base of the histogram (see illustration) to just inside the point where the graph ends. What this does is extend the tonal range to a point where the image is much improved.

Shifting the central slider adjusts the image brightness, or its gamma. This is a virtually lossless method of increasing, or decreasing, the image brightness. It's important to note here that most prepress professionals recommend that you perform any cloning/retouching operations after making these tonal changes—otherwise your brush/painting strokes might become horribly visible!

You can begin to appreciate the power of the Levels feature when these types of tonal changes are applied to a single color channel only. This gives the designer tremendous control over the final result (select the channel from the dropdown menu at the top of the Levels dialog box). Generally, single channel adjustments can be used for cleaning up color casts (white balance problems) in an image, or for creating really striking special effects.

50

1
The original image and its histogram, showing shadow (left), midtone (middle), and highlight (right) sliders.

2
Shadow slider moved to the start of the histogram, giving improved contrast range.

3
Dragging both the shadow and highlight sliders inwards produces increased contrast, burnt-out highlights, and blocked shadows.

4 | 5
Moving the midtone slider to the left or the right gives under or over exposed results respectively.

6
Moving the Output Levels sliders inwards reduces image contrast.

7 | 8
Adjustments can also be applied to individual color channels, as here to the red and blue channels. Note the differing histogram shape for the respective channels.

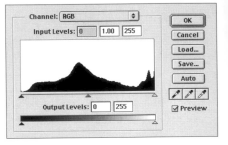

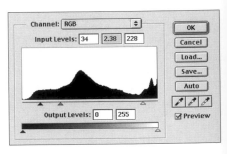

2

3

4

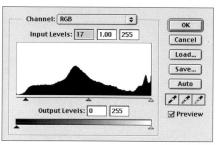

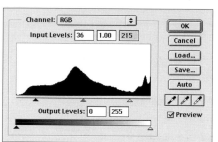

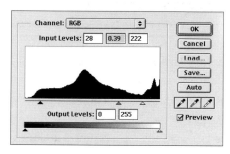

6

7

8

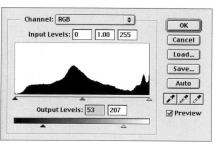

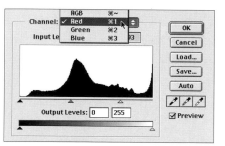

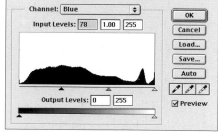

CURVES: THE ULTIMATE CONTRAST CONTROL

For total control over the color in any image use the Curves command.

Open an image and bring up the Curves dialog box (Alt/Command "M" or Image>Adjust>Curves, from the menu bar). The image tone is illustrated as an adjustable 45-degree graph representing a direct correspondence between input and output values. This offers a designer the ultimate in contrast and color control. As with the Levels command, the Curves feature offers first-time users a quick-fix "Auto" feature. For many poor-contrast shots "Auto" works quite well, though you still have little control over how much "auto adjustment" is added to the image.

But rather like the machine printing of films at your local photofinisher, this quick-fix feature makes certain presumptions about the image and, essentially, presumes that it contains an average range and dispersion of contrast levels. Though this is adequate for a surprising number of situations, it does not account for all. In these cases you'll have to use the Curves feature to make manual adjustments.

Open an image and click near, or on, the diagonal line. This produces a control point, which can then be dragged up, or down, depending on the degree and direction of contrast shift needed. The top right-hand portion of the line relates to the highlight values, while the lower portion of the line relates to the shadows. Note that if either end of this diagonal line is shifted to the vertical axes, the image data is "clipped" (i.e., it's permanently lost).

A normal contrast curve is slightly S-shaped, taking a form sometimes called an "Ogive" or "Ogee." Making

1
This is the Curves control panel as it is opened, showing a straight axis between the highlight (at the top) and the shadow to the bottom left.

2
Push the line down at its center to globally darken the image.

1

2

this adjustment requires three anchor points: one at the center of the line, one for the top of the "S," and one for the bottom. The more pronounced this "S" shape is, the heavier the contrast adjustment will be. As with the Levels command, you can apply these adjustments to a single-color channel only, in a range of color modes (or spaces), should you wish. A dropdown menu at the top of the dialog box gives you access to a chosen channel.

The great benefit of this feature is its color control. Curves allows designers to open particular color channels, adjust them with pinpoint accuracy, and then work on other channels, if necessary, before saving or making further adjustments to the gamma values. For example, daylight film that has been exposed in tungsten light might display an unwanted warm

(red/yellow) color cast. This can be removed by selecting the blue channel and placing the Eyedropper tool over the worst color-affected part of the image. Click in the image once to see where on the curve that tone appears. Then move the anchor point until you see the cast reduced. This takes some practice with a mouse—it's more accurate using a graphics tablet or actually entering specific output values into the dialog box provided. Use the latter option when you want to jump values in small increments. Color corrections usually require minute adjustments to the curve, while most special effects can be made with a much heavier hand. It is often faster and more accurate to produce color corrections in this way than by manipulating the three color sliders provided in the Color Balance dialog box.

53

3
Push the line up at its center to lighten the image globally.

3

4
Create a gentle S-curve to boost the contrast of the image.

4

COLOR-CORRECTION TOOLS

Photoshop, like all professional image-manipulation programs, offers a variety of additional color correction tools beyond Levels, Curves, and quick fixes.

In Photoshop, you will find these tools under the Adjust submenu under the main Image menu. One of the simplest is Color Balance, which is just one step higher than offering a quick fix. It lets you adjust the color content of an image based on perceived bias: for example, if you think the image is "too red," you can drag a slider from Red to Cyan to compensate.

For a more fundamental color change, try Hue/Saturation. Here you can shift the entire hue basis of an image so that the output spectrum is out of alignment with the input spectrum. This maintains a kind of color logic while adding a psychedelic touch. The control can also be used to increase or lessen the overall strength of colors in an image, which can be helpful for washed-out shots. Alternatively, if you want to change the hue, saturation, and lightness of just one particular color in an image, use the Replace Color function instead. It does the same thing, but limits which parts of the image are affected.

Subtler effects can be achieved with an expanded version of the Color Balance

2

Color Balance. Despite the simplicity of this control, the adjustments that Color Balance can achieve are often subtle. It's just a matter of dragging sliders from one color bias to its primary opposite, and applying this individually to shadows, midtones, or highlights.

3

Hue/Saturation. Note the two spectrum bars at the bottom of the dialog window: the change in hues is not random, but an ordered, logical shift of the output spectrum. Increasing the Saturation slider makes colors appear more intense.

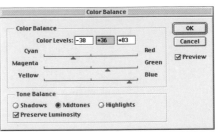

1

Shown here is the "target" image, allowing you to accurately assess what each of the color correction tools can do.

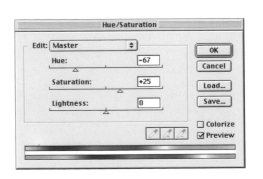

4
Using an Eyedropper tool, you click on areas in the image whose color you want to change. Then drag on the Hue, Saturation, and Lightness sliders, as with the Hue/ Saturation tool, to apply changes only to the color areas you have just selected. Here we used it to change the blue details in the clown's costume to green.

5
Selective Color. By altering the intensity of colors within the bounds of key primaries, you can make subtle changes without affecting everything in the image. For example, notice how the color shifts here have not affected the detail within the clown's white gloves.

55

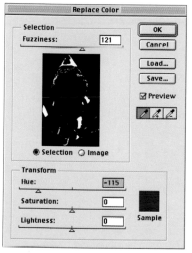

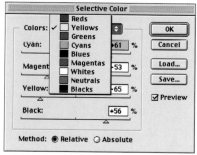

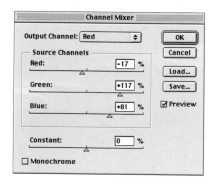

6
Channel Mixer. Visualize your RGB image as three grayscale channels, then imagine moving pixels from one channel to the other two. This is what the Channel Mixer is doing, letting you adjust the amount of image information from source channels to move to a selected output channel.

control, known as Selective Color. This provides a set of color intensity sliders, which apply within selective primaries and key color points: reds, yellows, greens, and so on. This allows selective saturation changes and primary shifts that won't affect everything else in an image.

Not-so-subtle effects are possible with the Channel Mixer. Since image manipulation programs generally define 24-bit color pictures as a combination of 8-bit red-green-blue channels, moving pixels between the channels can produce interesting results.

SELECTION TOOLS 1

All photo-editing programs include a range of image-selection tools. These are specifically designed to enable the user to isolate one part, or several parts, of an image so that he or she can apply a tonal adjustment, color change, or something more radical, such as a filter effect to part of the image only. Selection tools work in several different ways: as a Paint tool whereby you can use a brush shape to paint the selection (or "mask") over the image; as a Drawing tool whereby you can simply draw around the object area to be selected; or as a Color/Contrast tool, which makes a selection based on the color or the contrast of the pixels. Generally, one of these tools will make a nice clean selection. However, if the object to be selected is irregular in shape and tonality, you might have to use a combination of tools to make the perfect selection. These are typical selection tools:

Marquee Tool: used for drawing geometrically precise selections (e.g., this tool subset includes the "rectangular," "elliptical," and "single row/single column" marquee).

Lasso Tool: used freehand, like a pen. Its variations are the magnetic lasso tool and the polygonal lasso tool.

Magic Wand: this tool makes a selection based on the contrast of an image.

Making the initial selection is easy—just open an image, grab the appropriate tool, and execute a selection. For most jobs this rough selection might need refining—either by adding or subtracting a bit of the selection to make it fit "cleanly." This can be done using simple keyboard shortcuts. For example, holding down the SHIFT key when using any of Photoshop's selection tools adds to that current selection. Holding down the OPTION key (Alt key on a PC) subtracts from that selection. Selections can be saved for later use or feathered to soften the hard selection line (saved selections are stored as an individual monochrome channel in the Channels palette).

56

1
Picking out a simple area with one of the Marquee tools is just a click-and-drag operation. But it is not a very accurate tool, as you can see: precisely selecting the tomato alone is very difficult.

2
For a more hands-on selection, try the Lasso tool, which you use like a pen or brush to trace precisely around the area you want to select. You'll need a steady hand to achieve a precise result, though.

3
An easier alternative to the regular Lasso is the Polygonal Lasso. A series of clicks around an object is enough to surround it with a selection marquee with straight sides. Obviously, it's not ideal for organically shaped objects.

4
The Magnetic Lasso automatically locks onto the edges you want to select by distinguishing differences in color as you gently and slowly move the cursor around the object.

5

Photoshop provides vector-style Pen tools for plotting precise points, lines, and curves. The vector shape you draw can be saved as a named Path with the image, and subsequently used as a selection.

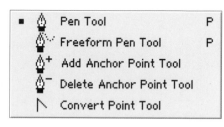

6

The Magic Wand tool selects areas in an image based on similar levels of brightness and color. By setting a tolerance value you can limit selection to those pixels with levels very close to the selected one or, by setting a higher value, to a much broader range of levels. Selection can also be limited to an individual channel.

7

By setting up an alpha channel mask, you can use Brush tools to paint over the areas you don't want. The remaining areas— shown in white— are then easy to select with perfect accuracy using the Magic Wand tool.

6

8

All selections can be "feathered," applying an anti-aliased smoothing to edges. You choose how deep the feathering should be (the radius), measured in pixels.

8

SELECTION TOOLS 2

Using a mouse to make your selections is OK, but it's even easier to use a graphics tablet. This device, though an expensive add-on, gives pinpoint accuracy when making any kind of manipulation.

Another way to get fast and accurate with a selection is to use Photoshop's quick mask mode. This feature converts the masked area to a Rubylith overlay (as in the old days when designers used to cut Rubylith masks on sheets of clear acetate when making up artwork). Everything that goes ruby-red in color will not be affected by any further actions. You can't actually do anything to the image while it's in this mask mode, other than top-edit the ruby overlay, but as soon as you flip back into standard edit mode again, the typical selection line appears and you can then apply your manipulation.

The ruby-red layer (the color can be changed) can be erased/expanded using any of Photoshop's excellent Paint tools—for example, the Paintbrush, Airbrush, or Pencil tools.

The keyboard shortcut for using this is, luckily, "Q," so it's easy enough to keep flicking backward and forward to see how accurately the selection process is traveling. The beauty of the Rubylith quick mask mode

3
Photoshop includes a dedicated cut-out selection utility called Extract. You start by using a highlighter-style Pen tool to trace around the transitional areas of your selection, which contain a mix of foreground and background—the frizzy hair, in this instance.

1
Selecting complex shapes with noncontiguous areas, such as the curly hair of this girl, is a job for more sophisticated tools than the basic selection set. The Magic Eraser works like the Magic Wand, except that it deletes selected areas immediately. This can work well when you want to pick out complex areas and see immediate results.

2
As mentioned on the previous page, painting a mask can often be the most accurate hands-on method of defining a selection. Using Photoshop's quick mask mode, where the mask itself appears as a ruby-red area over the top of your image, makes things clearer. But it's still not ideal for very complex shapes, as you can see.

4

Having designated the edge areas, you can paint in the solid internal area of your selection. This is easily done with a single click using the Paintbucket tool. You can now click on the Preview button to see how successful the automatic Extract function will be.

4

5

In this preview, the "extracted" areas are shown to be transparent, just as if you had used the Magic Eraser. But before committing yourself, zoom in and use the CleanUp and Edge TouchUp tools to correct any mistakes. Here, we're unmasking some hair that had been over-zealously extracted.

5

6

Click OK when you're happy to send the result back to Photoshop's main interface. For even more precise selection tools, for difficult images like this, you may wish to invest in third-party plug-ins such as Procreate KnockOut.

is that it's more stable to work with than a regular selection. Accidental keystrokes, for example, can't delete or lose the mask, whereas they might in the standard selection mode. It's also easier to fine-tune a quick mask using the Eraser or Drawing tool. If you have a graphics tablet, so much the better, as editing in this mode is faster and considerably more accurate than using a mouse.

The Eraser tool removes the semitransparent red mask. Note also that you can click back to standard edit mode to view the progress of the mask/selection at any stage. In some instances you might want to further modify the mask in this mode, rather than in quick mask mode, and then return to the latter state for further viewing or treatment.

As previously touched upon, all selections can be soft-edged or "feathered." This is an excellent technique to use because, if it's applied correctly, it brings a natural look to any selection by removing that "hand-cut" look that a lot of amateur selections tend have about them.

59

6

CLONING AND RETOUCHING

One of the most useful tools is the Cloning or Rubber Stamp tool. This allows you to copy-and-paste pixels from one part of an image to another, or even from another image opened in the same program.

The Clone tool is particularly useful for fixing tears, creases, and scratches in old or damaged pictures as well as for removing dust spots, chemical stains, age fading, and discoloration.

Cloning is also an excellent technique for combining more than one image in the same document producing a similar result to the more complex montaging techniques. This could be merging a small part of one image into another (for example, replacing detail in an eye) or combining several images onto a background using multiple layers and textures.

The Clone tool is controlled in a similar way to the Brush tools in a photo-editing program. The size of the area sampled from and pasted to is precisely editable using the edit function in the desktop palette. Options (using Adobe Photoshop) include soft- and hard-edged brushes, a variable clone source, and a range of different brush sizes.

4 | 5 | 6
Other Brush tools can be used for retouching purposes. Here we've used the Airbrush in Color Dodge mode with white as the foreground color.

Dodge helps to highlight detail lost in a dark image, while applying it with a brush allows more finite, localized control than a crass filter effect.

1 | 2 | 3
The Clone tool, called a Rubber Stamp in certain image-manipulation software, copies and pastes from one part of an image to another using brush strokes. It's ideal for retouching damaged photos or for removing unwanted detail.

60

6

5

Some tips for using the Clone tool are:

• Always perform your cloning operations on a layer copy. This gives the option of switching the effect on and off to compare it with the original layer.

• Vary the direction of the tool, the position of the clone source, and the size and opacity of its brushes. This will reduce the chance of making repetitious cloning marks, sometimes called "tram lines."

• Set opacity values to less than 50% (try 20 to 25%). This will slow down the process, but often produces a smoother-looking result. To avoid "tram lines" constantly change the clone source.

• If areas for "fixing" are soft-edged, select a soft-edged brush. A hard edged brush suits graphics and flat areas of continuous tone.

• With a large area to be cloned, draw around it using the Lasso selection tool and drag it to a good part of the picture. Select a suitable feather setting (try five pixels), press Command/Ctrl>Option/Alt to copy the selection, and shift it to cover the damaged part of the photo. Pressing Command/Ctrl "D" will deselect the cloned part of the image.

7 | 8 | 9

Switch the Brush mode to Burn when faced with an underexposed or generally pale image. This not only lets you darken and saturate areas with a painterly look, but also lets you create shading effects not in the original.

7

8

9

SHARPENING AND SMOOTHING TOOLS

Photoshop provides a number of dedicated Brush tools that can be used to paint particular effects on parts of an image. Most useful are the Blur, Sharpen, and Smudge tools.

With a simple click-and-drag motion, you can effectively paint Blur effects onto any image. This can be useful, for example, when trying to create a depth-of-field effect by blurring background areas to let a foreground object appear crisper. You can do this by playing with layers and selections, but just being able to paint around the bits you want blurred with soft- and hard-edged brushes is often faster and easier to control.

The Sharpen tool produces the opposite result, but should be treated with more care. While blurring discards image detail, you can't expect sharpening to generate detail that wasn't there to start with. Overuse of the Sharpen tool will lead to an ugly grainy effect.

The Smudge tool is more versatile than you might expect. As well as being an all-around retouching tool

1 | 2
Create a depth-of-field effect in order to prevent a background distracting from your foreground subject. But instead of tracing a complex selection or painting a mask before applying a filter, use the Blur tool to paint the blur effect directly onto the background.

3 | 4
Take a tip from magazine front covers: concentrate on eyes and teeth. The Sharpen tool is useful for making details like these brighter and crisper, making a good photo look even better.

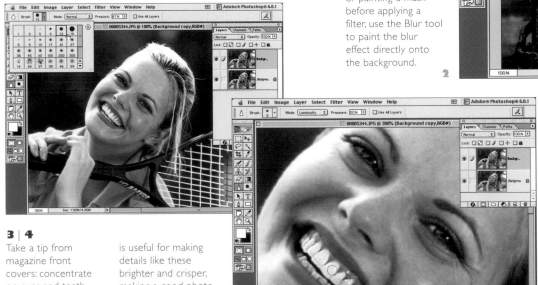

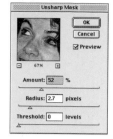

for covering up glitches with a little scrubbing action, the Smudge tool can be used as a hands-on directional blur tool. The Motion and Radial Blur effects under the Filter menu aren't controllable with the same immediate precision as a direct brush stroke.

The Filter menu contains a number of other effects in this category. Most notably, the Gaussian Blur produces the most realistic fuzzed-out blur result possible, akin to a lens defocus. In the same way, the most effective sharpen filter is Unsharp Mask, which attempts to sharpen edges and actual image detail rather than crystallizing all the pixels uniformly.

Also take a look at the Noise submenu under the Filter menu, because this contains several handy photo-retouching effects. Most notably, Despeckle and Dust and Scratches are helpful at cleaning up images with dirty surfaces or grainy film quality. One of the most unusual effects is achieved with the Median noise filter, which can produce a Gaussian-like blur but with crisp edges between color areas.

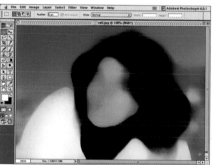

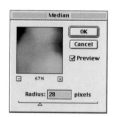

9 | 10
The best defocused lens effects are produced by the Gaussian Blur filter, also letting you adjust the spread of the pixel blur using a slider.

11 | 12
Median, one of the Noise filters, merges similarly colored pixels into each other. Increase the radius value to produce a unique blur effect, which maintains shape outlines.

5 | 6
Although the Smudge tool is good for eradicating small glitches, it can make a fun directional blur tool as well. With a few swipes around the London Eye, we can make it look as if it's positively spinning.

7 | 8
Always use the Unsharp Mask filter when crispening up a soft-focus image, since the plain Sharpen and Sharpen Edges filters are harsh, uniform, and uncontrollable.

63

USING LAYERS 1

Layers—and the Layers palette that displays and enables manipulation of the layers—are among the most important features in an image-editing application.

Image layers can be considered like transparent acetate sheets upon which image elements can be placed and stacked so that, from above—and along with the base, background layer—the composite image is visible. Other than the background, layers can be rearranged, edited, and even deleted. We can even use specialized layers—known as Adjustment Layers—to alter the characteristics of other layers.

Before the introduction of layers to image-editing applications, each artwork effectively comprised a single layer upon which all edits and manipulations were enacted. Once committed to the canvas, these edits were

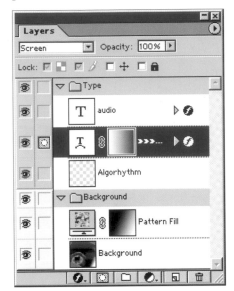

1
The Layers palette shows all the layers within an image stacked from the lowermost (the background) to the topmost, representing the front layer. Layers can be rearranged by selecting a layer and dragging it to a new position.

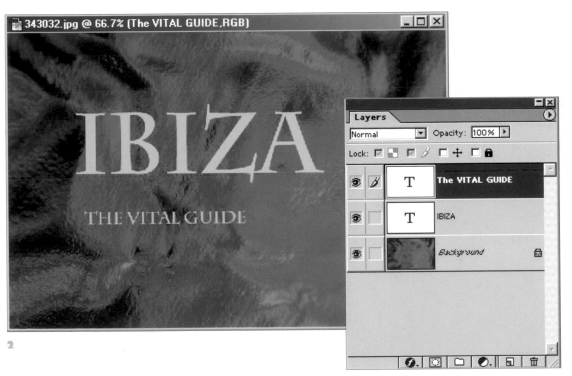

2 | 3
The eye icon to the left of each layer indicates layer visibility. Click on this to temporarily turn off the layer. Here the title text layer has been turned off in the second image.

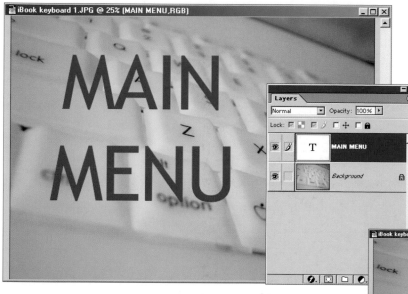

5 | 6
At the top of the palette are controls for the Blend Mode and the Opacity control. When a layer is selected, its interaction with the layer below is determined by the Blend Mode selected (see page 68). The transparency of the layer can be altered using the Opacity control. Set to 100% (the default setting), the layer is opaque; set to 0%, the layer is completely transparent. Here a text layer is shown at 100% (left) and 50% (below) opacity.

4
Icons along the base of the palette can be used as shortcuts for adding a Layer Style, a mask, a new set of layers, a new Adjustment Layer, and a new layer respectively. Dragging a layer to the trash icon permanently deletes that layer.

effectively "locked in." Should you have decided later that the application of a particular effect was inappropriate, there was little you could do other than start again.

The advent of layers has not only dramatically increased the flexibility of the way we work, but has enabled other effects to be created, such as Layer Styles (page 70) and Blend Mode options (page 68), which would otherwise be difficult to achieve.

New layers in an image can be created virtually at will, either as copies of the currently selected layer or as new, empty layers. We might want to create a copy of an existing layer, if, for example, we intended to apply an effect and combine this with the unfiltered version. An opacity control on the Layers palette varies layer opacity.

USING LAYERS 2

ayers—and layer features—can be used for more than
simple ordering and organization of image elements.
Using additional features, such as Layer Masks and
Adjustment Layers, we can add extra effects to our
images without irrevocably changing the appearance
of our image.

We can use Layer Masks when we want to make only
part of a layer transparent, or wish to vary the opacity of
a layer across an image. A Layer Mask is created by
selecting the Add Layer Mask option from the Layer
menu (or by clicking on the equivalent icon at the base
of the Layers palette). You can now use
the Airbrush tool (or any other painting
tool) to alter the opacity of the layer. As
you work you'll see the changes you
make indicated in the small thumbnail
next to that of the chosen layer.

Use black as the paint color if you
want to make areas transparent, and
white if you wish to increase the opacity
(you can use white to touch up any areas
that might have been made transparent
by overzealous use of black).

Adjustment Layers enable us to perform
manipulations on an image without permanently
affecting it. We can use these to make adjustments to
brightness and contrast, color balance, levels, and many
other image characteristics. These adjustments are then
enacted on the layer—or layers—below.

Once we have created an Adjustment Layer it can be
turned on or off just like any other layer. Consequently
the effects of the Adjustment Layer can be turned on or
off, too. Should we determine later that the Adjustment
Layer is no longer required, we can even remove it.

3
Painting with the
Airbrush tool (in
this case) renders
part of the layer
transparent (and
bordering regions
semitransparent).

4 | 5
Shift-clicking on the
Layer Mask icon will
(temporarily) disable
it and restore the
image to its original
state. Pressing Alt
and the Layer Mask
icon (Windows), or
Option and the Layer
Mask icon (Mac), will
show the mask on the
full-screen image
(useful for fine-tuning
the selected area).

1 | 2
This image comprises
a layer and the
background. We can
add a layer mask to
the layer by clicking
on the Layer Mask
icon. Our selection
is confirmed by a
thumbnail that
appears next to the
layer thumbnail. (The
linked chain icon
between the two
indicates that the
layer mask is linked
to this layer.)

1

3

66

7

Depending on the type of adjustment layer you select, a corresponding dialog box will appear. For example, selecting Color Balance will open the Color Balance dialog box. You can then make alterations to the settings as if you were doing so to the image itself.

8

Once you have created an adjustment layer you'll see the familiar Layer Mask thumbnail alongside that of the Adjustment Layer. You can use this to gain precise control over the layer. Painting with black, for example, will mask out areas and protect them from adjustment, as in this background.

 67

6

Add an Adjustment Layer by clicking the icon on the Layers palette. The options for your adjustment layer will appear in a popup menu (you can also select New Adjustment Layer from the Layer menu).

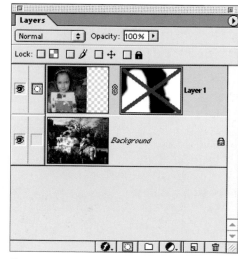

ABOUT BLEND MODES

Blend Mode options appear frequently in Photoshop and other image-manipulation applications (where it is sometimes called Merge Mode). A Blend Mode describes the way in which a layer, or a painting tool, interacts with a layer below it or the background.

Adobe uses the following convention, which has now been adopted more widely, to describe blending.

Base Color: the pixel color in the Lower, or Background, Layer. It is the original color of the image.

Blend Color: the pixel color being blended from the Blend Layer, applied using the Painting or Editing tool.

Result Color: The pixel color that results from the blend.

In most cases, transparency can be altered in a blend to reduce (or intensify) the effect of the blend.

Here's how the different Blend Modes affect Base and Blend Colors. If the descriptions seem a little obtuse, refer to the illustrations. These can often give a better indication of the practical effect of the blend.

Normal (default mode): Depending on the transparency used, Base and Blend Colors are combined directly.

Dissolve: Base and Blend Colors are combined to give the result color, but in a random "spatter" pattern.

Multiply: Multiplies the Base Color value by the Blend Color value to produce a color that is always darker than the original.

Screen: Multiplies the inverse of the Blend and Base Colors to give a lighter result.

Overlay: Multiplies or screens colors dependent on the color of the base.

Soft Light: Darkens or lightens color dependent on the Blend Color. A light Paint or Layer Color lightens the Base Color, a dark one darkens the Base Color.

Hard Light: Multiplies or screens the colors depending on the Blend Color to give a spotlight effect. Contrasts tend to be emphasized and highlights exaggerated.

68

Base Image

Paint Layer

Screen

Overlay

Color burn

Darken

Hue

Saturation

Normal

Dissolve 50%

Multiply

Soft Light

Hard Light

Color Dodge

Lighten

Difference

Exclusion

Color

Luminosity

Color Dodge: Analyzes the colors in each color channel and brightens the Base Color depending on the Blend Color (note that blending with black produces no change).

Color Burn: The opposite of Color Dodge.

Darken: Compares color information in each channel and selects the darkest of the Blend or Base for the result.

Lighten: The opposite of Darken.

Difference: Subtracts the Blend Color from the Base, or the Base from the Blend, depending on which is brighter.

Exclusion: Produces a similar result as "Difference," though lower in contrast.

Hue: The hue of the Blend Color is combined with the luminosity and saturation of the Base Color.

Saturation: Combines the saturation of the Blend Color with the luminosity and hue of the Base Color.

Color: A result color is produced from the hue and saturation of the Blend Color and luminosity of the Base.

Luminosity: The luminosity of the Blend Color is combined with the hue and saturation of the Base. Other Blend Modes are possible, and are included in some applications.

69

LAYER STYLE 1

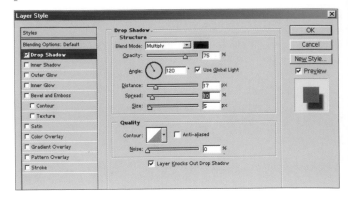

Layer Style comprises one or more layer effects that are applied to a layer in an image, and create an interaction between the contents of that layer and the underlying layer. Perhaps the most common and obvious Layer style is the Drop Shadow. When a Drop Shadow is applied to a selection in a layer, a shadow is cast on the Background Layer, visually suggesting that the selection is suspended above the background. This is a useful device for adding depth to text that has been added to an image.

Each Layer style features a dialog box that controls the parameters of the effect. For example, in the case of the dropped shadow, we could define the position of the shadow. Do we want the shadow to imply a light source above or below the selection? To the right or the left? Do we want a crisp shadow (which might be cast by a point-light source), or a softer one (simulating the effect of hazy sunlight)? We could, if appropriate, set the color of the shadow.

Layer Style can include any one (or more) of the following effects.

Drop Shadow: The shadow we've just discussed, which falls behind the layer selection.

Inner Shadow: A shadow is applied inside the layer selection, giving the impression that the selection has been cut out from the background.

Outer Glow: A glow that radiates outward from the selection boundaries.

Inner Glow: A glow that radiates inward from the selection boundaries.

Bevel and Emboss: Adds bevels and emboss effects (we will look at this more closely later).

Color, Gradient, and Pattern Overlay: Used to overlay, respectively, a color, gradient, or pattern on the selection.

Stroke: Uutlines the selection boundaries using a color (or, alternatively, a gradient or pattern).

1

The Layer Style dialog box for Drop Shadow. In the Structure panel we can set parameters relating to the size, extent, and angle of the shadow. Our adjustments are displayed on the thumbnail to the right. We can also set a Blend Mode (sometimes called a Merge Mode) to determine the type of interaction between the effect and the background.

2

Preset Layer styles can be dragged and dropped to a selection. This is often the most expedient way to apply compound Layer styles that comprise multiple effects.

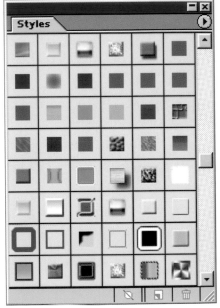

In some applications these individual effects are combined into preset Layer styles that can be applied directly to a layer selection. These may be grouped together in a palette, or accessible via a menu selection. Typically these are designed to create specific customized effects.

70

3

4

5

71

6

7

8

3
This image comprises a textured background and a type layer. We can apply Layer styles and observe the results.

4
Drop Shadow. The opacity has been set to 60%, and the size to 28 pixels.

5
Inner Shadow. Increasing the size of the shadow increases the perceived depth of the effect.

6
Outer Glow. For clarity, a red color has been selected for the glow.

7
Inner Glow. Again, a red color has been used to show the glow effect.

8
Emboss. This simple embossing gives the appearance of letters raised above the background.

9
Gradient Overlay. A standard rainbow overlay has been used here.

9

LAYER STYLE 2

Layer styles are useful in creating Web page elements. In particular, the Bevels and Emboss effect is used extensively for creating buttons, controls, and other interface elements. By altering the parameters in the dialog box we can simulate effects such as a button being depressed, which comes in useful when creating rollovers. In such situations we may use three Layer styles. The first will simply display (for instance) a button. The second will show that button highlighted. This version of the image might be used when a mouse rolls over the button. The final style will show the button depressed. This would appear when the user clicks the mouse over the button, and provides visual feedback that the button has been "pressed."

Note that Layer styles can be applied to any layered selection. Hence, when creating Web page elements, don't feel constrained to stick with the conventional rectangular or circular forms when, for example, creating buttons. Depending on the nature of your work, it might be more appropriate to make the elements you use reflect the content. Creating these effects is easy; the process is outlined in illustrations 4 to 7.

72

1 | 2 | 3
One button, three looks. These are the representations of our button for the three states outlined in the text—the button default, the button responding to mouse rollover, and the button depressed.

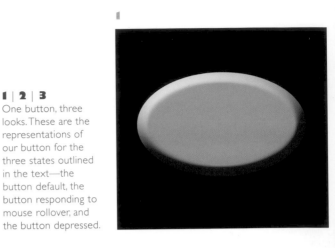

4 | 5
Create a new layer in your image and draw your button shape. This could comprise a selection filled with a color, or (as here) a vector shape. Apply an Emboss Layer Style to give the button a 3D appearance, as in illustration 1.

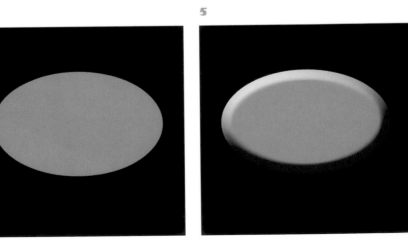

6

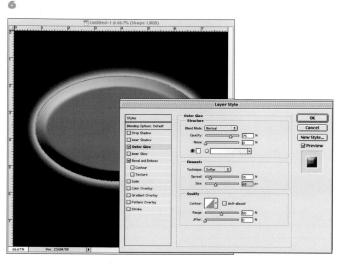

7

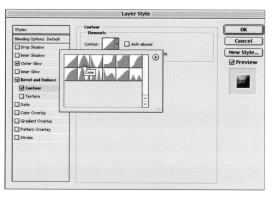

8

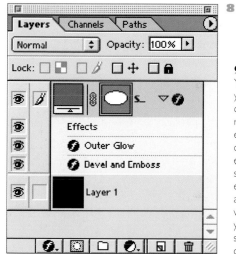

6
Select Layer Style and add an Outer Glow. Use your own judgment to determine the size and scale of the glow effect. We are aiming here to give the button a highlighted effect. This is our second state.

7
Select the Contour option from the Layer Style dialog box. This gives us the means to modify the shape of the emboss. Selecting this cone shape gives a depressed look to the button. You can enhance the effect by reversing the direction of lighting on the button.

8
Note that the Layer styles are indicated in the Layers palette (here, in Photoshop). Where compound effects have been applied, each is shown individually. Should you need to remove effects, they can be dragged individually to the Trash icon.

9 | 10 | 11
You needn't confine your buttons to conventional rectangles and ellipses. Layer styles can be applied with equal effect to any shape. Here, the effects have been applied to preset vector shapes, but you could employ the same method to your own shapes.

9

10

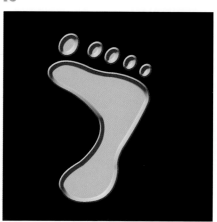

11

FILTER EFFECTS

Image manipulation programs always come loaded to the gills with a range of weird and wonderful filter effects. These are essentially the digital equivalent of placing a special effects filter over the lens of your film camera, except that the range and depth of digital effects are far greater than any analog camera could achieve.

Filters are actually incredibly useful, more perhaps in the process of creating something else than in the straightforward applications that analog filters were designed for. Like all other actions, filters can be applied to a selection only—the eyes of a portrait, for example—making them an powerful addition to any designer's creative palette.

Most filters are variable—that is, you can increase the component actions of each filter to fine-tune the end result and save that effect as a special action for later use. This is essential if you're running similar effects over a range of Web navigation buttons and bars, for example. As well as existing as standalone effects in their own right, most designers use software filters in combination to give a far more accomplished effect.

Here are 25 possible filter effects—just a small sample of what is available.

Original Image

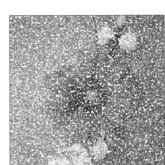

Colored Pencil

Crosshatch

Ink Strokes

Mosaic

Pointillize

Graphic Pen

Water Paper

Craquelure

Patchwork

74

Dry Brush

Film Grain

Paint Daubs

Plastic Wrap

Spatter

Solarize

Mezzo Tint

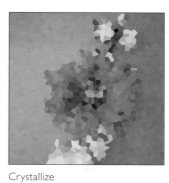

Crystallize

Lighting Effects

Lens Flare

Chalk and Charcoal

Conte Crayon

Extrude

Tiles

Spherize

Wave

VECTOR GRAPHICS

Though most digital imaging involves pixel-based representation, vector graphics provides an alternative.

Image manipulation applications work on the fundamental basis that an image is made up of pixels—discrete elements of finite size within an image. When we manipulate an image we make changes—individually or collectively—to the pixels of that image. We do not change the pixel structure in any way. Such images are described as "bitmapped."

A particular manipulation may involve drawing a shape on our image. Though this may be a complex selection-based shape, let us consider adding a straight, diagonal line to our image. If we examine this line in close-up by zooming in on our image, we will see that our line has been applied by "coloring in" the original pixels that lay in the path of the line. The more we zoom in on the line, the more ragged and pixellated it becomes.

76

1 | 2
This digital image appears continuous until a small section is enlarged. Then its pixel-based nature becomes obvious. Were we to want an enlargement of a small section, the pixels would be obvious and the quality would be unacceptable.

3
A circle drawn on a canvas in an image-editing application appears to have a well-defined edge.

4
Again, when enlarged, the pixel-based nature of the shape becomes obvious.

Vector graphics, the form of graphics that is most often employed by illustrative software, use an alternative method of representation wherein every shape, curve, and line is represented by a mathematical function. The benefit of this representation is that an illustration or image can be scaled in size without becoming degraded. If we were to zoom into a shape created using vector graphics, we would find that, even with very high magnifications, the boundaries of that shape remain crisp and precisely defined. This also applies to most patterns and gradients: as we change the scale, the patterns used to fill will be rescaled accordingly. Only "fixed" elements will not change. For example, if we have specified a boundary line as being 1⁄16in wide, this will remain constant no matter how large or small the illustration becomes.

Though it is broadly true that image-manipulation software uses pixel-based representations and illustration software uses vector graphics, many applications in each category can handle illustrative elements of the alternative type. Hence, vector graphics can successfully be used in Photoshop (although possibilities for vector editing are limited), and Deneba's Canvas integrates vector and bitmap graphics in a single application.

5
A similar circle drawn in a vector-based application appears equally sharp as the pixel-based image when viewed at large scale.

6
When we enlarge the circle this time, the edge remains sharp and well defined. The mathematical expression that describes the circle enables it to be reproduced at any scale with identical resolution.

7 | 8
In this piece of vector graphics artwork, each element (including textures and fills) is expressed mathematically. The component paths that comprise the final artwork can be seen in the second illustration.

7

8

5

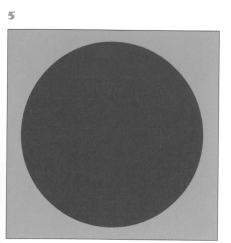

6

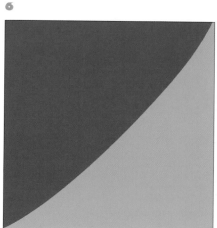

WORKING WITH TEXT AND IMAGES

Take care to keep text readable. Even after years of experience it is easy to use text colors that don't read over an image. Choose images carefully and, unless you are confident that you know your target audience, only combine them with text overlays if the result is readable on a wide range of machines.

No Web site is effective if built on text alone, just as few sites include nothing but images. Interestingly, more and more splash pages are being designed using only images or animations. Thankfully the "this is the home page for…" opener is long gone. Text will not be discussed at any great length here, as this is a book about images; however, it's worth mentioning the proliferation of text animations that are currently flooding the Internet—either as introductions to sites, or as components of sites.

Many designers choose to integrate text with an image, and then convert that to become an interactive part of the site. For example, a user will click or mouse over a button and a text instruction appears. Using images, you can animate a photograph to reveal text, other photographs, and even other page links. This is

1 | 2 | 3 | 4 | 5 | 6

When working with text it is essential to remember that legibility is affected by the background. Here the text color and the background color are too similar, resulting in text that does not stand out. Too much of this and your visitors will go elsewhere. This dark blue on yellow is a much better choice for legibility. Generally speaking, textured or patterned backgrounds are to be avoided, especially with fine text. Text on very fine or soft textures can be readable. Placing a solid block of color behind a headline can avoid texture and color clashes. Drop shadows are another simple solution to ensure that text stands out.

78

1

2

3

4

5

6

called an "image map." You can also "program" a photograph to change into another image as a user moves his or her mouse over it—an "image swap." Images can also be animated to change into several different states as the mouse rolls over, clicks down, clicks up, or moves off the original position. This is called a "rollover," and is usually applicable to buttons and other navigational aids.

Basic text animations are not only easy to construct (*see* Section Five: Dynamic Image Content), but they also change the animated text into an object, with the result that the user can both read the content and immerse him-or herself in the visual metaphor created by the animation.

This is also relevant for images. A moving image, in the form of an animation component or even a tiny animated GIF, attracts the viewer's attention and focusses him or her on the message, whether an advert, a product, or another part of the site. Text and image animation, therefore, are powerful tools to have built into your site. However—and this applies to most things related to good design—don't overdo it.

79

7 | 8 | 9 | 10 | 11
This animation sequence created by the Swedish Web designer Daniel Achilles (www. precinct.net) is an excellent example of how text can be used in an imaginative and creative way. As the size of the circle increases we get to see the whole picture, visually and metaphorically.

HTML TEXT AND GRAPHICS TEXT

Using HTML coding to produce text that will be displayed on a Web page has advantages. It occupies a small amount of file space, and downloading is swift. It also assures consistency: subject to the vagaries of browser customization, the text should be reproduced pretty much as the originator intended.

However, though we can change the size, color, and—within a limited range—the font, there is little more we can achieve with HTML text. If we want to create a unique headline, use non-standard fonts, or add embellishments such as layer styles, we need to resort to graphics-based text. As a graphic, we can manipulate the text at will, using any of the tools from our image-manipulation application. We must be mindful, though, that as a graphic, the resultant file is likely to be substantially larger than an HTML equivalent. Hence, unless there are exceptional circumstances, we should restrict graphic text to limited elements of our Web site.

When we add text to an existing image or graphics file (or if we are creating a new file from scratch), the

1
Adding text to a file is simple. You need only select the Type tool and enter the text.

2
As with a word processor, you can then select some or all of the text to make changes. For example, you can correct spelling mistakes, and even change the layout, using justification tools.

3
Because type is written to a new Image Layer, Layer Styles can be applied to add emphasis to the text. It is worth noting, however, that adding effects can add additional colors (such as a range of neutrals in a Drop Shadow) to an image. This can increase the file size and introduce non-Websafe color. This can be significant if your image will ultimately be saved as a GIF.

5

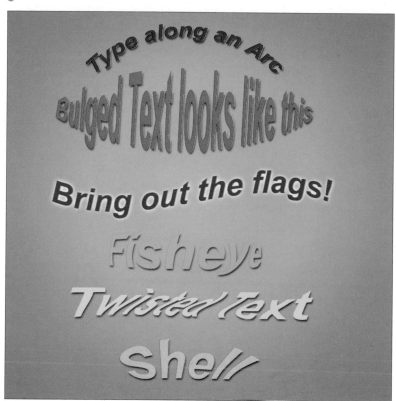

4

Text can be written vertically by selecting the Vertical Text button on the Tool Options bar.

5

Type Masks permit the outlines of the type characters to be used as masks, and images (or other graphics) to be placed within. This can be very effective, but can also introduce additional colors that will later compromise the degree of optimization that can be achieved.

4

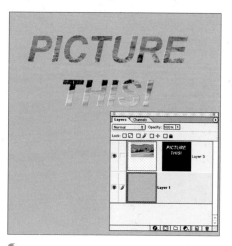

6

6

Photoshop features a range of Text Warp effects that are easily applied to selected text. Text can be distorted using one or more of these features.

text is written to a unique Type Layer. As with other layers, we can return to it later and edit it, perhaps changing the wording or the font, or even rescaling and applying a new effect. As the conversion of a layered file to a Web-compliant format results in the loss of layer editability, it is wise to keep a copy of the file in the application's native format (PSD in the case of Photoshop), in case we need to make changes.

Graphics and illustration software, such as Macromedia's Freehand or Adobe's Illustrator, can be used to create even more advanced and complex text effects. Should you have the need, you can create your text with these and export the file in a Web-compliant format (or in a format acceptable to your image-manipulation application). If you do not have access to an illustration package, don't worry. The latest Photoshop versions (including Elements) include comprehensive text manipulation features.

UNDERSTANDING RESOLUTION

Resolution is not as big an issue for Web designers as it is for those working in print. For a start, all Web images are limited to a device resolution of 72 dots per inch (dpi), the resolution of a computer monitor. For this reason, software features—like Adobe Photoshop's excellent "Save for Web" feature—automatically convert every file from its original resolution to 72dpi.

In the course of building a Web site, you'll have to deal with a great many file types and file resolutions. All of them need to be converted before displaying on the Web. It's always a good idea to keep your master files at their maximum output dimensions until you have a good idea of the size at which they are to be run on the Web. There's little point in saving all the files as 150 x 280 pixel images if some will be needed at a larger size at a later date. For photographic images, it's always far better to manipulate or color-correct a larger image, and to downsize it only when it's placed in the Web application.

When preparing images for the Web, the workflow should go something like this.

Digitizing: Scan all non-digital source material in-house (if you have the facility), or by outsourcing it to a bureau.

Build a Master File: Make all your scans 300dpi. However, there is little point in making a 100%-sized scan from a quarto-format artwork; you'll never display it like that on the Web. Work within the parameters of the display medium (i.e., 800 x 600 pixels, or—just to be on the safe side—1024 x 960 pixels.)

Save As: Save these scanned files, in a non-lossy format, such as TIFF, into your master folder in the root directory.

3

1 | 2
Converting the resolution of an image from the typical 300dpi used for printing to the screen resolution of 72dpi can compromise image quality, particularly when the image contains diagonal lines and rectilinear forms.

3 | 4
The degradation due to the reduced resolution is more obvious when we examine a section of each image. Though the pixels are visible in the 300dpi file, they are all too obvious in the 72dpi copy.

1

2

4

5
Changing the resolution in the Image Size dialog box will have no effect on the size of the image. Ensure the Constrain Proportions box is checked, maintaining the ratio of height to width when either dimension is adjusted.

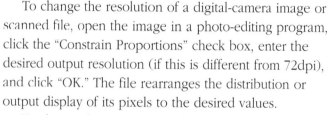

Image Size

Pixel Dimensions: 12.4M
Width: 2400 pixels
Height: 1800 pixels

Document Size:
Width: 33.333 inches
Height: 25 inches
Resolution: 72 pixels/inch

☑ Constrain Proportions
☑ Resample Image: Bicubic

OK
Cancel
Auto...

5

Pixel Dimensions: 792K (was 12.4M)
Width: 500 pixels
Height: 450 pixels

6
You can use the dimensions in the Pixel Dimensions box (in preference to the physical Document Size dimensions) when aiming to fit an image to a screen size.

6

7 | 8
A Web image may need to be resized in order for it to be easily accommodated in a browser window. Here, an image is shown in a browser at the original dimensions. Resizing enables it to be viewed without scrolling.

8

To change the resolution of a digital-camera image or scanned file, open the image in a photo-editing program, click the "Constrain Proportions" check box, enter the desired output resolution (if this is different from 72dpi), and click "OK." The file rearranges the distribution or output display of its pixels to the desired values.

To change the output size of a digital-camera image or scanned file, open the image in a photo-editing program, click the "Constrain Proportions" check box, enter the desired output dimensions, and click "OK"—or, if you're going to manipulate the image, select dimensions that are larger but closer to the final output size. For example, if you think the final dimensions are going to be around 175 x 88 pixels, enter 250 x 150 pixels and change the image size after the manipulation process. I suggest this primarily to make the manipulation process faster—if you use a program like Adobe Photoshop and try to work with a 1200- x 800-pixel image, it may take forever to redraw in each optimizing window. A 250- x 150-pixel image redraws almost immediately.

CREATING WEB-SAFE COLORS

As briefly mentioned in the first section, not all color is Web-safe. This is because the Web, for all its power and pervasiveness, is still restricted to a limited color range. For this reason, all graphics have to be converted from RGB or CMYK to Indexed Color space. The initial translation limits the bitmap image or vector graphic to just 256 colors; this can be further reduced in the conversion dialog box to Web-only, which uses just 216 colors. Some graphics might not look any different when converted to this color space (it is the default color space for the GIF file format), but others might change quite drastically. If this happens, there are a number of things that we can do to limit the damage to the appearance of the file. These include dithering, a process whereby textured "noise" is added across the image in an attempt to break up the color patching or blotches created by a limited color range. Changing an image from RGB to Indexed Color often replaces smooth tonal gradations in the image with noticeable, hard-edged bands of color, with no gradation at all. This effect is called "posterization." Your job is to try to reduce the posterization effect as much as possible.

84

2
Zooming in close to one of the optimized images shows how the colors are dithered to create intermediate tones.

Original Image

128 Colors

1
Here is an original image, and copies that use a steadily decreasing number of colors. In each case, dithering is used to simulate "missing" colors. As the number of colors becomes progressively smaller, the dithering is less successful at producing semi-continuous tones. Previews such as this are ideal for making direct comparisons between images before optimizing an image for the Web.

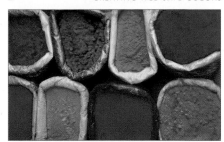

Locking-off Colors

One advantage the GIF file format has is that you can lock-off colors. What this means is that you can effectively select the colors you must have in an image, and then remove much of what is left to reduce file size and decrease the display time. Again, Photoshop's Save for Web function does a good job of this by displaying the range of indexed colors in use in its color table. Simple graphics can be reduced to extremely small file sizes in this fashion with no loss of detail or quality. JPEG equivalents, of course, are poor in comparison—but this is not surprising, as JPEGs are better suited to preserving tonal gradation in an image, while GIF files are more suited to graphics that contain little or no tonal gradation.

3 | 4
When you create a GIF file, you can select how many colors an image contains and reduce the image to that number of colors to give a more compact file size. However, automatic color reduction can sometimes remove colors that are important to the image. This image has been reduced to 16 colors with the loss of some of the principle tones.

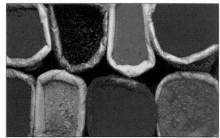

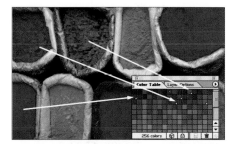

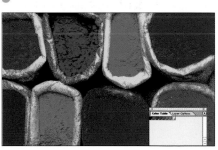

64 Colors

24 Colors

5 | 6
Where it is important to retain a specific color, it can be identified on the color table using the Eyedropper to select the color on the image. By clicking on the padlock symbol, that color will then be used as one of the reduced color set. Here, with only eight colors selected, the tones (if not the detail) remain authentic.

85

OPTIMIZING WEB IMAGES

The real dilemma, when making or preparing images for the Web, is how much quality to sacrifice against the speed with which the page will be displayed. Most Web designers will go for speed, knowing full well that a page that takes a minute to display is about 50 seconds too long for most viewers. One day, all consumers will be armed with broadband connections that will allow us to add richer quality and content to our sites. Until then, we have to learn to optimize!

What exactly is optimizing? Simply put, it is the software-based technique that's used by all Web professionals to get the smallest possible files while sacrificing as little quality as possible.

Adobe Photoshop, among others, has a highly efficient Save for Web option (in its File menu), which is specifically designed for optimizing files for the Web. On a base level, it's quite intuitive to use and includes a quadruple-image-view window option that allows you to compare four versions of the same image under different optimizing criteria. The beauty of this is that not only can you compare different JPEG compressions at the same time, but you can also change one (or two, or all of them) to a GIF file for an instant face-to-face comparison.

I

Crop as tightly as possible around your graphic in order to keep the file size as small as possible. When creating Web graphics in a vector illustration package, group the objects and use the grouped selection as the crop.

2 | 3 | 4 | 5 | 6

GIF file sizes can be significantly reduced by "locking" the important colors in the image while discarding the rest. In this example, a 16-color, 3.76Kb GIF has been progressively reduced until just two colors remain. The progressive removal of colors isn't always obvious until you reach just six, although this depends on the nature of the image being optimized.

10-color GIF • 3.36Kb   8-color GIF • 3.16Kb

Here's how to optimize a file for the Web.

• Open the file and make sure that the resolution is set to 72dpi.

• Change the file's output dimensions to match the published dimensions.

• Don't save the file, but instead select the Save for Web option. The image is opened in the optimizer window. Select either full-page optimizer view, 2-up, or 4-up. I favor using the 4-up option, because it gives you a better range of "visible" options.

• Select the file format you want to save to—GIF for vector graphics, text, type, and images with a lot of flat color in them; JPEG for just about all photographic images that contain a lot of smooth tonal gradations.

• Settle on a compression amount that you are happy with. The window displays the time each compression version will take to download using any of the preset modem speeds.

• Click on "Save" and save the image to its respective file folder within the site's root directory.

7 | 8
As you can see from this example, although the JPEG file format (bottom) clearly wins out in terms of reproducing tonal gradations, GIF files (top) are ideally suited for graphics, as they produce cleaner-looking backgrounds and less obvious image artifacting. Size is also important here: if the graphic is to be reproduced at a small size, there's no point in trying to reproduce a tonal gradation that will be invisible to the eye!

7

8

87

6-color GIF • 2.57Kb   4-color GIF • 2.02Kb   2-color GIF • 1.70Kb

IMAGE COMPRESSION

Image compression is an essential part of the digital imaging business. Most images intended for Web display need to be compressed so that they can be downloaded quickly. Also, if you are buying a digital-still camera for producing quality Web site images, be aware that most models are sold with only a low-capacity removable memory card (currently 16Mb or 20Mb). These are too small to hold many digital images, especially if you choose the higher quality settings.

Can any file format be compressed? The simple answer to this is "no." All digital cameras now offer the user at least two file formats in which to save their photos. One will be an uncompressed file format like TIFF or RAW, and the other will be the JPEG format, which can be compressed to a variety of quality settings. TIFFs are both "lossless" (they can be compressed and not suffer any quality loss), and readable by a wide variety of software programs, which makes this format a good option if you want to squeeze the last drop of quality out of a digital camera's resolution.

The JPEG (Joint Photographic Experts Group) file format is a "lossy" format: even on its highest quality setting, it will lose some picture quality, though this may be imperceptible to the naked eye. The lossiness isn't an intentional part of the compression technology so much as a side effect that worsens as compression increases. Most image manipulation software allows you to set the trade-off between file size and image quality, since some images survive the compression better than others. An advantage of using JPEGs is that they are totally cross-platform—any computer can read a JPEG file. Also, JPEGs compress so well that dozens more images can fit onto a removable memory card than would otherwise be possible.

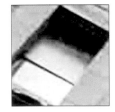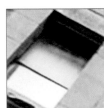

JPEG high
compression

JPEG low
compression

Uncompressed tiff

This shows you the kind of image degradation to expect from a JPEG file saved at the | highest compression (low-image quality), compared to how it appears when saved as a JPEG saved at its | lowest compression (high-image quality), plus the same image again as a non-lossy TIFF file.

2

3

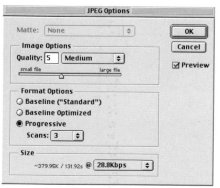

2 | 3
Though saved at the same compression ratio, these two pictures with identical dimensions and resolution produce quite different file sizes when compressed. Smoother, less cluttered tones like those on the right, produce considerably smaller files than those that are busy and full of detail. In this case the difference is 380k compared to 104k JPEG file.

IMAGE SLICING

Image slicing is a tremendously versatile technique that, as the name suggests, involves converting large, relatively unwieldy graphics into fast-loading, neatly-designed Web pages by cutting them into slices. Aside from the obvious advantages of having a faster-loading page, image slicing allows you to design a Web page in its entirety (rather than in bits using Dreamweaver or GoLive), and then to optimize that in one go.

The idea with slicing is to isolate different sections of the image so that they can be individually optimized to suit. Headers, logos, and other pieces of text can be sliced for optimizing as GIFs for flat color and graphic logos, JPEGs for sections with photographic content, and so on.

A Web page can be sliced into an infinite number of slices, and each slice can be optimized at a different compression setting. Additionally, a Web page need not be entirely sliced; that is, a designer might only slice the important parts and leave the background. Adobe ImageReady, for example, then decides how to deal with the rest of the un-sliced page for you.

On a more advanced level, a Web page that has been designed as one unit can be optimized using any masks that have been created within that document. You might, for example, create a channel mask to select a particular product or logo in a page. This can be saved as a channel (as you would any mask), and then optimized at a different setting to the rest of the (unmasked) image. Not only can you select different JPEG compression levels using channels, but you can also vary the amount of dithering, lossiness, and color reduction in a GIF file. This technique is called Weighted Optimization.

1

2

1
An image slice can be created on any image by dragging the Image Slice tool from the top left to the bottom right of the intended slice area. Slices created in this way are known as User Slices. Additional slices (known as Auto Slices) are created to in-fill the surrounding area so that every part of the image is enclosed by a slice. Different colors indicate Auto Slices, User Slices, and the currently active slice.

2
Drawing a second User Slice on the same image results in a modification of the arrangement and number of Auto Slices.

3

Taking this Web page graphic as an example, we can use the Slice tool to divide the image into discrete areas that might later be used for particular Web features (such as rollovers and hyperlinks).

4

We begin by selecting the large graphic. Because this could potentially lead to a large file size, we can optimize this separately from the rest, using a higher compression ratio.

5

Now we can slice each of the menu items. The nature of the slicing tools is such that they tend to snap to each other automatically. If you want to ensure precision you can use the guides to set up a framework for the slices.

6

In the finished page, Auto Slices have been created in those areas we have not sliced. We can now, if we wish, optimize each slice individually. This is particularly useful in situations where it is important to preserve detail in part of an image but less so elsewhere. We then get an image that is optimally compact.

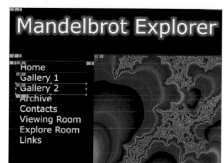

Image Slicing Basics

Here is a basis step-by-step guide to image slicing.

Step One: Design a Web page. The beauty of image slicing is that you can create this using any software: graphics, illustration, photo manipulation.

Step Two: Open the completed page in Photoshop and drag guides (View>Show>Guides) across the image to act as a visual guide for the Slice tool.

Step Three: Cut the full-page graphic into slices using the Crop tool—take care to label each section correctly so that, when you reassemble the image as a table, all the pieces end up in the right place.

Step Four: In your Web application, create a table with the same number of cells as there are slices. Drag each sliced image into its respective table cell. Make sure that each cell is the same size as the image section/slice. If the page looks misaligned in a browser, check to see that all alignment directions are valid for the images (i.e., "top," "bottom," "center," "left," "right," and so on).

Photoshop's Image Slice tool permits an even higher level of sophistication. When you cut up an image using this tool, Photoshop automatically saves each user-defined slice as its native state (rollover, animation). Anything that's not specifically selected is automatically saved as an Auto Slice. Auto Slices automatically link together and are regenerated every time a user-defined slice is created, edited, or changed. You can easily convert Auto Slices to User Slices so that their properties are preserved.

You can also pre-select the content of the image slice depending on whether it is an image or a flat color. This is another way to optimize the download speed of the entire page. All slices run at full-page optimization unless you specify otherwise. You can also create a background color to ensure that the text, for example, appears perfectly matched with other graphics within the image.

IMAGE MAPS

An image map is a powerful design tool that can be used in situations in which regular (rectangular) image slicing won't work. Image maps are also easier to create, can bring simple interactivity to a site quickly, and can be integrated into the general navigational structure of the site.

On a basic level, an image map is an image that has a series of embedded links (Hotspots) to other documents or Web sites. When a user moves his or her cursor over a Hotspot, the cursor will typically change from a pointer to a hand, thus indicating a link.

An advantage of image maps is that they can be made into irregular shapes, and so they are ideal when the desired Hotspots overlap each other or are irregular in shape (you can overlap multiple Hotspots). Aside from being a useful design tool for navigational features, image maps can be used for entertainment, and as such are popular in kids' sites as a "discovery" feature.

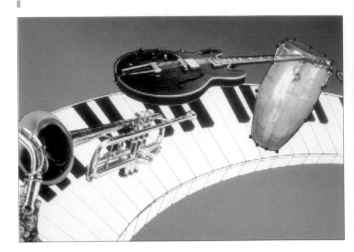

1

The Polygon Image Map tool enables the creation of image maps of almost any shape. This tool works broadly in the same way as the Polygonal Lasso: the edge of the image map is selected by clicking at points around the perimeter (unlike the Polygonal Lasso, absolute accuracy in defining the edge is not required). Click at the start point to "close" the image map.

2

Additional image maps can be drawn on the image. In this case the guitar map overlaps that of the drum. While this is permitted, overlaps should be used sparingly as there can be a risk of erroneous selections when hyperlinks are assigned to each map.

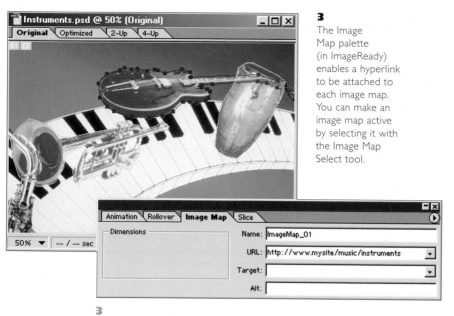

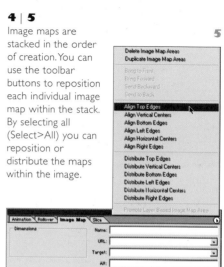

3
The Image Map palette (in ImageReady) enables a hyperlink to be attached to each image map. You can make an image map active by selecting it with the Image Map Select tool.

4 | 5
Image maps are stacked in the order of creation. You can use the toolbar buttons to reposition each individual image map within the stack. By selecting all (Select>All) you can reposition or distribute the maps within the image.

6
Though image maps are essential for creating shape-based selections, they often provide an expedient (and alternative) method of creating active areas of a more conventional shape. Here, the Rectangle Image Map and Circle Image Map tools have been used for these buttons.

When you make an image map you can edit the size and shape to fit the image exactly—it is a very versatile feature. In Dreamweaver, an image map is simply created by opening a page, choosing the Hotspot tool from the properties inspector, and drawing the Hotspot over the selected image. At any stage this can be changed, edited, or deleted. The Properties dialog box offers an Alt field (for adding an alternative title in text if the image is slow to load), a Link field (to describe where the image map is to look for the linked page), and a Target field (in which you decide whether a new page should open or not). You can use this technique on photos and graphics within an existing HTML page. Adobe ImageReady is able to handle entire Web pages as if they were complete photos. Image maps can be created by simply drawing a suitable Hotspot on the background layer, or they can be applied to a separate layer and optimized as elements that are separate from the background.

WEB ANIMATION AND VIDEO

There is no doubt that even a modest animation on a Web site can enliven that site considerably. Web animations tend to fall into one of two camps: GIF animations and Flash. It is, as we have already seen, a property of the GIF file format that it supports animation. Like the animation in TV and movie cartoons, GIF animations comprise a series of frames, each slightly different from the one that precedes it. The practicalities of downloading files over typical Internet connections restrict the scope of GIF animations, so that they are comparatively simple.

GIF animations can be created either from a series of frames, or by using a document with separate layers that can be turned on or off to create sequential frames.

Creating a GIF animation (or, indeed, other animations) is made more simple by a process known as "tweening." When the Tween command is invoked, a new frame can be created between two existing ones by interpolating the changes that occur between them.

1
Several image-manipulation applications provide the tools to build GIF animations. This is the Animation palette from ImageReady. Here we have created a simple graphic comprising a circle in the first frame and a block in the second.

2
Invoking the Tween command (in this case, from a button on the palette) enables a smooth transition between the two original frames. We can set the number of new frames to be added and how long each frame remains visible. We can also configure the animation to play once or continuously.

3
Proving that GIF animations are not the poor relations of Flash, Web sites such as Smash the Status Quo! (www.smashstatusquo.com) act as showcases for the capabilities of the format, and for devotee designers.

96

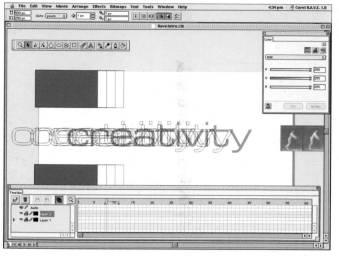

The other major Web animation format is Flash. Although file sizes are typically larger than those of GIF animations, Flash animations provide for enriched graphics and high-quality animation. Flash was devised by Macromedia, though some other applications can produced animation that can be exported in the Flash format. ShockWave, also from Macromedia, enables applications created in that company's Director to be embedded in a Web page.

Compared to animation, videos on the Web are generally a lot more demanding of bandwidth. But, given the increasing number of users connected with fast, high-bandwidth, broadband Internet connections, movies downloaded from a Web site or streamed from a remote host are an increasingly practical resource.

97

4
Corel's RAVE provides particularly elaborate tools (that in many ways mimic those of digital movie editing) for the creation of elaborate animations. The results can be exported as GIF animations, QuickTime movies or even Flash animations, as here

5 | 6
Similarly, Adobe's LiveMotion allows the creation of advanced animations (which can included effects drawn from Photoshop), and multiple tracks, as this timeline demonstrates. The finished animation can be output as an optimized SWF Flash file.

7
Digital video has given us simple but powerful movie editors such as Windows Movie Maker and Apple's iMovie, shown here. Movies can be compiled from a range of sources and then saved in one of a range of formats. At the moment (due to speed considerations), only the most compact are suitable for Web projects.

WEB ANIMATION AND FILE FORMATS

The beauty of GIFs and Flash is that they can produce effective animations from files that are compact enough to be downloaded to a user's browser without undue delay. Downloading video material in the same manner is more problematic. The amount of data required to display a video is substantially higher than for an animation. But this has not prevented the development of compression regimes that enable video replay. In some cases, this requires a large file to be downloaded. In others, a process known as "streaming" is used, wherein a file is partially downloaded (sufficient for a few seconds' worth of replay, enough to "buffer" the movie), and replay begins immediately. By matching the amount of material downloaded to the buffer to the speed of the connection, the video should play without interruption to the end.

Let's now take an overview of the principle formats for Web animations and video.

Animated GIFs

The format in which GIF animations are stored is both convenient and compact. It also benefits from being one of the fundamental file formats, namely GIF, that all browsers are capable of displaying without ancillary plug-ins or add ons. It is easy to create GIF animations even if, ultimately, they lack the flexibility of other formats.

Portable Network Graphics

The PNG format was originally devised to circumvent the proprietary nature of the GIF format. Animation of a similar type and quality to GIF animation is possible (animated PNG files are known as MNGs), but the PNG file format is not supported by all browsers (though it is typically the older, less-used browsers that do not).

1
The QuickTime player supports a range of file types on Macintosh, Windows, and Unix Platforms.

2
SVG content allows instantaneous updating or live changing of graphics.

2

SWF Files

This is the ShockWave Flash format. As we have already seen, Flash is capable of elaborate animation effects with file sizes that are only moderately larger than those of a typical GIF Animation. ShockWave permits a greater level of animation (and interactivity if required). In order to view Flash animations, a Flash plug-in is required. A ShockWave plug-in, necessary to view ShockWave content, will also permit viewing of Flash animation.

SVG—Scalable Vector Graphics

The name of both a file format and a Web development language, based on the HTML extension XML. High-quality graphics can be produced that contain real-time data (for example, weather forecast graphics can display current weather details). Viewing SVG content requires an SVG viewer. These are downloaded to browsers but are also provided with many (particularly Adobe) applications.

AVI—Audio Video Interleave

The standard for video (and audio) on Windows computers, but viewable on other platforms (with, for example, QuickTime Player). AVI files can be compressed for Web dissemination.

MPEG—Motion Picture Experts Group

A family of formats designed for the distribution of video and audio content over a range of media. MPEG1, the original format, was designed to permit the encoding of full-screen video at VHS quality on a conventional CD (the video CD standard). MPEG3 is the higher-quality format used for DVD video. The audio component of MPEG3 is better known as MP3.

QuickTime

QuickTime is the de facto standard video replay on Macintosh computers, but it is also available on other platforms. This is a scaleable format that enables videos of up to 640 x 480 pixels at 30 frames per second to be displayed (though this size is unlikely to feature on Web-page video). QuickTime players support a number of other video file formats, including MPEG. A QuickTime extension, QTVR, permits viewing of immersive panoramas (*see* page 108).

Real

A format used mainly for streaming video to a RealPlayer. Quality is on par with AVI, though quality can be increased or decreased depending on the speed and efficiency of the connection. The RealPlayer can be downloaded to replay this (and other) file formats.

99

3

4

3
ShockWave content can be complex and interactive, such as here with the popular PhotoJam.

4
RealPlayer provides replay of downloaded and streamed video files.

GIF ANIMATION

There are several production tools on the market, including simple but effective shareware packages such as the famed GIF Construction Set, dedicated GIF production programs like Ulead's GIF Animator, and companion products like the much-acclaimed ImageReady package, which comes as an added extra with recent releases of Adobe Photoshop. All programs provide the user with the ability to create and sequence individual images or frames. Most also contain built-in compression features that allow you to preview your completed animation with different color and frame-rate settings. More recent releases include a small but very handy device that predicts the file size of the previewed

1

1 Individual artists, as well as whole companies, now specialize in creating GIF animation for the Web industry. ©Peter Andersson and ARG! Cartoon Animation, 2001, USA.

2

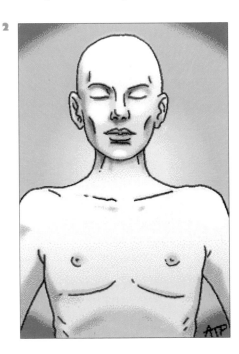
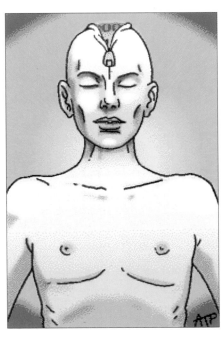
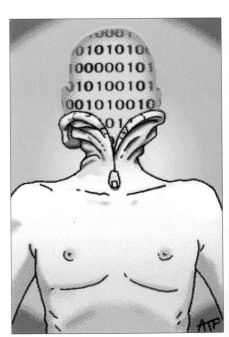

3

animation, and estimates its download time at different modem speeds. For those looking for an all-around 2D animation tool, some of the more sophisticated options provide the ability to output complex productions as QuickTime or AVI movie files.

Designers new to the area should try a range of packages before settling on the one that suits them best. All the major manufacturers of GIF animation software provide some type of "try before you buy" system. Check the Web sites, as these "demo" versions are usually available as downloads.

Compactness is the key to good Web animation. The Web is not the right place to try to achieve full, life-like motion in your animations. Most successful GIF creators manage to isolate the key movements that are essential to portray the motion of objects, and they use these as the basis for the animation. In addition, these designers also restrict the color palette of their compositions. Often, what seem like quite complex productions will contain fewer than 10 frames and 16 colors.

To get you started, look carefully at the banner ads next time you visit a busy commercial site. Download the GIF files of examples that you feel work particularly well, and view the frame sequencing by importing the file into your GIF software. Keep in mind, though, that just like all the other images on the Web, GIF animations are someone's property, so you cannot use them without permission.

Adobe has combined the Layers feature in its Photoshop, or PSD, format with the frames concept used for GIF animation. In Elements and ImageReady, there are options that allow the user to convert each layer to a separate frame in an animation. Making your first production is as simple as cutting and pasting graphic elements onto several different layers, making the position of the main components slightly different from one layer to the next. The image is then saved as a PSD file and opened in ImageReady.

101

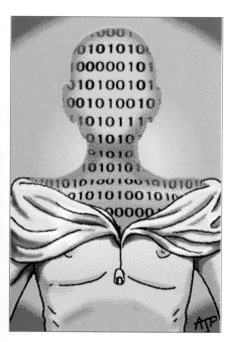

2
Some digital artists use the GIF format to produce art-based animations for the Web audience. ©Aidan Potts, 2001, UK.

3
An animated GIF contains a series of images or frames that are displayed one after another in a quick sequence to portray movement. ©RW, 2001, USA.

THE SIMPLE ROLLOVER AND IMAGE SWAPS

Things that seem like second nature to us now were not even possible a few years ago. The simple rollover button is a great way to attract attention to your site. When the viewer's mouse pointer moves over the button, the image changes. Such a response to a viewer's action gives a feeling of interaction to the site. A simple idea, but the underlying technology took a few years to develop. Most recent releases of Web-page construction and image-editing software contain built-in features that make producing these buttons easy. Programs like Adobe's ImageReady allow the user not only to set up the picture that will be used for the button, but also to write the special code that is needed to make the button work.

As the button is essentially two separate images that are displayed at different times, the first step in the process is to create the graphic for the button when it is in the "normal" state, and a second graphic for when the mouse pointer is over it. These pictures are usually the same size, but this doesn't have to be the case. For our example, the "normal" image is a simple rounded rectangle outlined and filled in ImageReady. On a separate layer, the word "rollover" is added and made

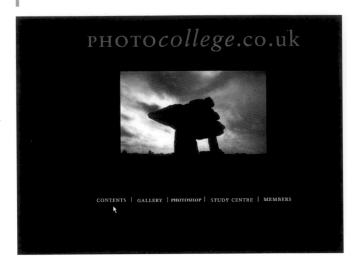

1 | 2
The top image of a rollover button changes when the mouse pointer moves over it.

3 | 4
With Adobe's ImageReady program, it is possible to create the images and text used for a rollover button, as well as the underlying code that is needed to make it function. Create the graphics for both the normal and "over" states of the button.

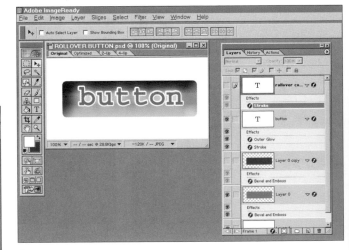

4

3

102

2

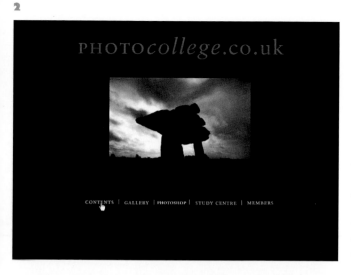

more graphic with the help of some layer effects. Both layers were then copied and used as the basis for the "over" image. The colors of the button and the text label were then changed.

With the base images complete, the Rollover palette was opened. With the normal state selected, the text and image layers were made visible by clicking the eye icon. A new state—the "over" state—was then made, and the button and text label for this layer were made visible. The palette provides a preview of how each state will look. The final step in the process involves saving an optimized version of the button as an HTML file that can then be viewed in any browser.

5

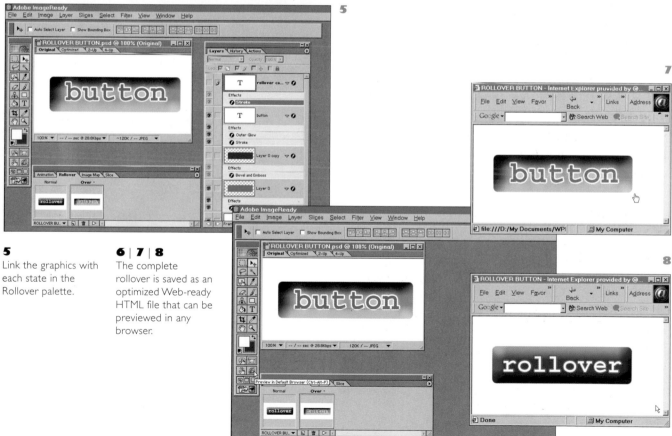

5
Link the graphics with each state in the Rollover palette.

6 | 7 | 8
The complete rollover is saved as an optimized Web-ready HTML file that can be previewed in any browser.

7

8

6

FLASH ANIMATION I

Flash is the biggest thing to happen to animation on the Internet since the Web was just a twinkle in Tim Berners-Lee's eye.

The key to Flash's success is that its propietary file format (SWF) uses vector graphics (see pages 76 to 77). Because vector graphics files are so much smaller than bitmap equivalents, it is possible to create really striking animations that still keep within the boundaries required for quick downloading and viewing times.

In addition to small file sizes, Flash animations only store the key frames of movement rather than all the images, as is the case with GIF.

The Flash program has quickly outgrown it's "just for animation" tag, and is now used to create fully functioning, image-rich sites, complete with navigation systems and information pages. The package dominates the market so much that in recent years other manufacturers have brought out packages that output to the Flash format. In particular, Adobe's Live Motion and Electric Image's Amorphium software both output to Flash. The SWF format has become the default standard for 2D animation; however, unlike GIF formats, Web surfers still need to download a plug-in for their browsers to view Flash-enabled sites.

ShockWave, *originated (like Flash) by Macromedia, is a technology that enables versions of multimedia material created in Macromedia Director to be delivered over the Internet to a Web browser. ShockWave material tends to involve more interactivity than Flash, but the dividing line between the two can be fine. ShockWave content can be produced in Flash (the application), but requires a browser plug-in for viewing. Web pages containing ShockWave content are often described as being "Shocked."*

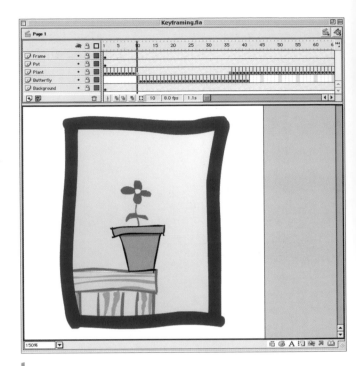

1

2

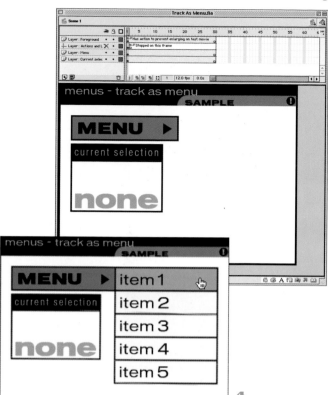

4 | 5
Once you have constructed your graphic, the Test Movie command compiles your work and offers it up as it would appear in a browser. Here, an interactive menu similar to that in PhotoJam (see page 99) is being tested.

6 | 7
Similarly, more complex interactive ShockWave features—such as this desktop calculator—need to be tested prior to deployment on a Web site. "Test Movie" compiles the project into a Flash file and makes it available for testing.

6

1 | 2 | 3
Flash provides a timeline that ensures pinpoint accuracy in both position and timing. The frames can be positioned so that actions (such as the interplay between the flower and butterfly here) can be precisely aligned.

3

7

FLASH ANIMATION 2

Those users who are familiar with one of Macromedia's other products, Director, will feel quite at home using Flash. It has the same look and feel as the company's premium multimedia product, and—in fact—the program started life here.

The best way to think of Flash is as two tools in one: a drawing tool and a movie tool. The toolbar that is displayed when the package is first opened will contain many familiar icons. Most of these are common to all drawing packages, whether they are vector- or bitmap-based. The image window associated with most graphics packages is replaced by the "stage." It's here that the Flash images are drawn. A second window contains the Timeline. This is in place of a series of frames found in a lot of GIF animation packages. The motion and movement of picture parts in your Flash movie are controlled with the Timeline feature. The frames in the Timeline that contain blue dots are called Key Frames, and are the pivotal point for action and motion changes.

The components of your movie can be drawn with the tools in Flash, or imported from other vector drawing programs such as Illustrator and Freehand. Despite being a vector-based program, Flash can also be used to import bitmapped images for your production.

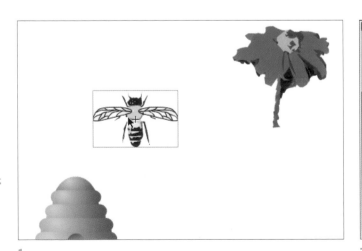

2

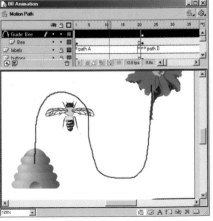

1

2
The animation is created with the bee in a separate layer from the other graphics. Begin by selecting this layer and adding a Motion Guide (Insert menu >Motion Guide).

3
We can now describe our S-curve, setting fixed Key Frames for the motion.

1
Object motion is a feature of all animation types, but motions are often limited to straight lines. Flash allows the easy creation of more ambitious movements. Here we'll use Flash to move this bee from the hive to the flower, following a broad S-curve.

At the beginning of most movies, a set of blank frames are made in the Timeline. A Key Frame is inserted at the beginning and end. With the first Key Frame selected, images can be drawn or imported onto the stage. Select your graphic and choose Insert>Create Motion Tween from the menu. Next, click on the last Key Frame and click and drag the picture parts from one part of the stage to another. When you play the movie, a slider moves across the frames from left to right. As this occurs you will notice the objects moving from their first position to the one selected in the second Key Frame. Unlike most of the GIF animation products we looked at before, there is no need to draw every single frame in the animation. Once the Key Frames have been composed, Flash draws the frames in between. This process is called Tweening.

Other important Flash concepts are Symbols and Libraries. Flash saves space within its movies by only storing re-used objects, or symbols, once. The symbols are stored in a library associated with the movie, and can be used many times in multiple frames without adding to the file size. It's important to remember that drawn objects are not automatically stored to the library as symbols; this is a separate process.

Just as with Photoshop files, the Flash environment uses layers to help separate and control different movie elements. Each layer is shown in the Timeline window.

When it is finished, the Flash movie is saved as a SWF file. The file is then placed—using Web layout software—onto a page, and saved as an HTML file. As SWF isn't natively supported by Web browsers (yet), anybody wanting to view a Web page containing your Flash movie will have to download the free plug-in from the Macromedia website.

The basics, as outlined above, make the Flash system seem like a simple animation environment. This is far from the truth, as there are many dedicated users whose work is highly complex and original. The sites that they create provide audiovisual experiences that are not equalled anywhere else on the Web. The Flash gallery on the Macromedia Web site is a good place to visit, as it will provide you with a list of sites designed to show off the power of the package.

4 | 5 | 6

By placing the bee on the start of the path, and using the Flash Tween command, the bee will be drawn at interpolated intermediate positions, following the path both in position and, as shown here in mid-flight, in orientation.

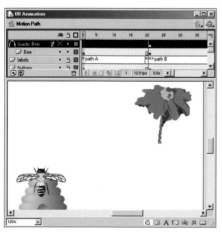

4

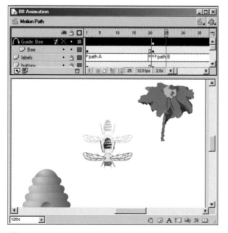

5

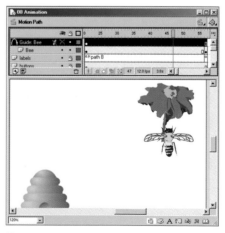

6

107

PANORAMAS

Panoramas have long been part of the landscape photographic tradition. Bulky swinging-back cameras, swinging-lens cameras, and even rudimentary cut-and-paste techniques have been employed to deliver the wider view.

Digital photography gives us the opportunity to create wide (or, equally, tall) views by digitally combining individual shots. The results can be equally impressive whether printed (special over-long panoramic media are available for many printers) or viewed on-screen. Such images can even be used on Web sites, thanks to Apple's QuickTime VR (Virtual Reality) format. Using VR, you can move around the panorama, with the option of zooming in and even jumping (via a hyperlink) to another scene or area.

Panoramas, whether conventional or VR, make intriguing and potent additions to Web sites, and are remarkably easy to create.

Compiling a Panorama Sequence

First create a panorama. Virtually any camera can be used to generate the source images. For best results, it should be mounted on a tripod, and the tripod head levelled with the horizon. Take a series of still photos with an overlap of around 30% between adjacent shots. To prevent uneven lighting effects it is usually desirable

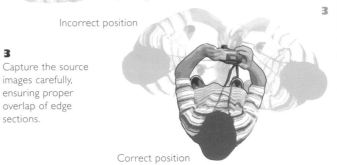

2
Incorrect position

2
When capturing handheld-source images, ensure that you pivot around the camera, not around your body.

3
Capture the source images carefully, ensuring proper overlap of edge sections.

3
Correct position

to use a fixed exposure time and aperture (either by setting the camera to manual, or by locking the exposure). The number of exposures required to describe the panorama will depend upon the focal length of lens used.

Building the Panorama

Software capable of creating panoramas (a process known as "stitching") ranges from simple stand-alone applications—such as MGI's PhotoVista—through to

1
QuickTime panoramas can be viewed interactively, allowing the audience to look right and left as well as up and down—all with a few simple mouse moves and clicks.

1

4

5

Import the source images into the panoramic program. Stitch and edit the sequence. Output the finished image to a QuickTime VR format, which can then be viewed in any VR-enabled Web browser.

dedicated VR applications. Some image manipulation software (for example, PhotoSuite from MGI and Photoshop Elements) includes panorama-building features. PhotoSuite is also suitable for image quilting, a process by which images can be stitched horizontally and vertically.

Images are imported into the appropriate application in sequence. There are then several options. Do we want a full 360-degree panorama or a lesser one? Do we want the image overlaps to be blended? We can also use manual intervention to position images if the automatic stitching routine is unable to create an exact match. In many applications, it is also important to enter the focal length of the lens that was used to take the individual photos. This ensures that the subsequent panorama build is free of distortion.

Creating a VR Panorama

If you want to create a VR panorama, you will need to save the result in QuickTime VR format. The file is then added to a Web page using layout and production software, and the finished production can be previewed in a QuickTime-enabled browser.

Creating the panorama can take some time, so it is useful, where the option is available, to run a preview

stitch first. This assembles the panorama at low resolution and without the full stitch. It is ideal for assessing whether the images are correctly arranged and aligned. The full stitch should produce a seamless blend of all the images. In practice (and because a wide range of exposures may be involved in a 360-degree panorama), you may need to perform some remedial work in an image-manipulation application.

Cubic Panoramas

Rather than sitting back and complacently enjoying the explosion of panoramic images hitting the Web, Apple has recently released a new version of its QuickTime viewer that can be used to view cubic panoramas. This new format allows the viewer to look up, down, and around themselves as though he or she is standing within a sphere.

Unlike traditional panoramas—which make the viewer feel as if he or she is standing in the middle of a cylinder that has scenery painted on the inside—cubic panoramas position the viewer inside a ball. At the moment, not many software packages are available that perform multi-image cubic stitches, but as the demand for this imagery increases, more commercial products will make their way onto the market.

PUTTING MOVIES ON THE WEB

Like 3D graphics, movies take up huge amounts of storage space and delivery bandwidth. Yet, despite these problems, Web video technology has been steadily developing and improving over the last few years. Again, companies like Apple provide the lead with media viewers such as its free QuickTime package. The key to videos on the Web is the strength and quality of the compression system, or CODEC, used to squeeze the massive amount of data contained in every second of a movie into a form that can be delivered to your desktop and displayed within a reasonable download time.

Early versions of the technology required the whole file to be downloaded before any of the video could be viewed. Recent advancements in streaming (see page 98) allow the first part of the movie to be displayed while the rest of the file is still downloading. This means that the Web audience is watching your production instead of waiting for it to start.

As with still-image editing, there are a host of editing packages that are designed to source, enhance, cut and paste, and produce movies. From the most simple and easy-to-use entry products like Ulead's VideoStudio, through to full-broadcast-quality production systems such as Adobe's Premiere, these programs enable users to sequence a series of video clips and sounds, before outputting it back onto tape or disk.

Most video-editing packages have the facilities in their post-production features to output to file formats that are suitable for Web delivery. The technologies vary, but all applications reduce the size of movie files by compressing the information, reducing the color set or

1 | 2 | 3
Several different plug-ins are available to enable browsers to display the videos contained on Web pages.
5) Windows Media Player showing the movie in WMV format.
6) QuickTime Player showing the movie in cross-platform MOV format.
7) Apple's QuickTime viewer embedded in a Web page, displaying the video compressed for Internet delivery.

4 | 5 | 6 | 7
Video-editing software ranges from simple icon-driven packages to full-broadcast-level programs.
1) Ulead VideoStudio
2) Adobe Premiere
3) MGI Videowave
4) Studio Basic for RealVideo

110

2

3

111

frame rate, and making the display size smaller. It takes a fine balance of these factors to achieve a production that is both watchable and deliverable.

The future of good Web design will involve the inclusion of a range of multimedia and dynamic content in pages and sites. The limitations of current bandwidths and delivery formats still determine how much of this technology makes it to viewers' screens, but so-called broadband connections are now reaching consumers' homes in large numbers. It won't be long before a rich audio-visual experience on the Web becomes the norm rather than the exception.

6

7

BEYOND THE TWO DIMENSIONS

Though 2D animation has the lion's share of the Web market, there are a few exciting and innovative 3D products that are finding their way into the Web community. Simple effects that give added dimensions to text headings can be handled by products such as Xara3D and Ulead's Cool3D. Most full-object or environment-animation projects are handled by traditional 3D animation programs, such as 3DS Max and Amophium, which are then ported to the Web.

As the demand for 3D animation for the Web grows, the software manufacturers have responded by providing GIF, QuickTime, and SWF output options for their mainline products. Simple rendered headings or small spinning animations are usually saved as natively supported files such as GIF, whereas complex 3D

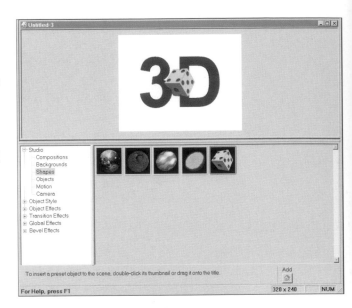

1
Major 3D rendering programs have the ability to port their content to the Web, but the viewer's Web browser will still need to contain a specialist plug-in.

2
Add text and pre-designed or imported objects to the work area.

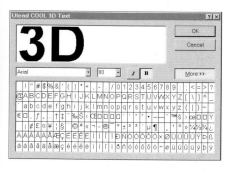

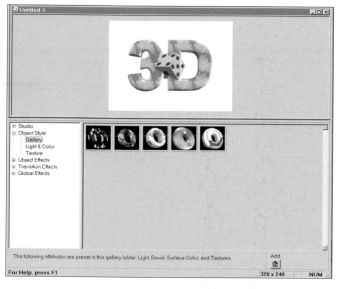

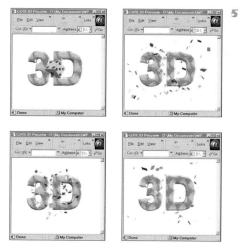

3 | 4 | 5
Apply color, texture, and animation type to the text and object. The final animation is output to either GIF or video format so that it can be easily integrated into a Web-page design.

and interactive, immersive-environment games a more realistic option. As things stand at the moment, the lack of delivery speed is the major obstacle that is holding back the greater use of 3D interactivity on the Internet.

Making a Simple 3D Animated Heading

Constructing simple 3D animated headings is less complex than it used to be, thanks to a range of dedicated step-by-step software programs that are designed specifically for the purpose. Text is entered directly into a word-processor-type dialog box. Properties such as texture, color, and bevel can all be altered interactively, and—finally—a pre-designed motion can be added. The final production can then be saved, either as an animated GIF file or in one of a range of video formats, such as AVI.

When used carefully, the output from these products can add 3D interest and movement to Web pages without the need for the designer to learn complex rendering programs.

environments that contain sophisticated lighting, reflection, and texture effects typically use a movie file format complete with specialized compression, such as MPEG. To achieve true 3D-environment interactivity, Web browsers need to be empowered with extra plug-ins. At the moment there is no one clear leader in the field, and the manufacturers are all trying to gain enough market share to make their plug-ins the default industry standard.

All 3D files are big, but as greater numbers of Web surfers choose to speed up their Internet delivery by subscribing to cable or DSL services, the increase in available bandwidth will make complex 3D Web sites

113

WEB-DESIGN SOFTWARE

There is an immense range of software available for creating Web sites. Simple shareware solutions enable the launching of simple Web sites at minimal cost. Some hosting services offer online or CD-based design products as part of their package of hosting your site. These products are often ideal for the newcomer to Web-site design, as they tend to have a very formulaic and step-by-step design approach. Because of this the results can often be very proscribed and, in offering a limited or rigid range of tools and features, may compromise the aims of the creative user.

More extensive and flexible products tend to command premium prices, but are nonetheless essential to the serious Web-site designer. Twin pillars of this world are Adobe's GoLive and Macromedia's Dreamweaver, upon which virtually all the significant Web sites we would care to browse have been conceived. Like most contemporary products, these are fully WYSIWYG—what you see is what you get. That is, designers can now lay out the components of pages in much the same fashion as they do when creating layout spreads for a magazine, using page layout software.

1

2

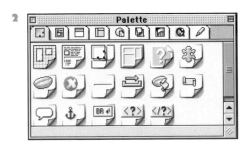

2
Another advantage of a high-level site-building application is the ease with which page resources can be assembled onscreen.

The use of drag and drop routines makes it simple to add a feature (from a range of presets) or create your own from scratch.

3
Though the interface differs, Macromedia's Dreamweaver offers a similarly comprehensive specification. Web pages can be built and consolidated and components created in Flash or ShockWave can be imported and added to a page.

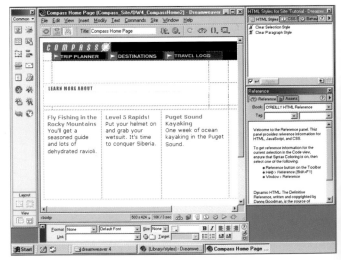

3

116

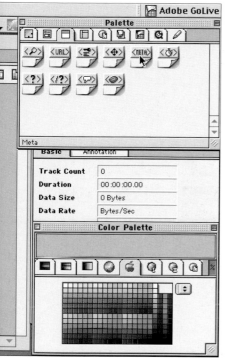

1
GoLive makes it easy to construct an integrated Web site in which all the assets—the Web pages, HTML code, and media—are managed. This makes it difficult (though not impossible) for a user to create a mechanically deficient site. Though no software can improve poor graphics or design elements, GoLive can ensure that site links and sequencing are valid and complete. Assets can be laid upon the workspace in the same way as they will appear through a browser.

To users of Photoshop and ImageReady, GoLive has obvious advantages because there is a considerable compatibility of functions and styles between the two. Though the imaging products from Adobe feature extensive specifications, the point will soon be reached when you will need to collate your pages in a dynamic multidimensional array through which your visitors can navigate easily. GoLive offers automatic asset management in which all your separate pages, their interconnections, and hyperlinks—along with other media files—are tracked and monitored for integrity.

GoLive, like Dreamweaver, will also allow access to potent Web features not available (or not feasible) in image-editing applications. Dynamic HTML, cascading stylesheet templating, and support for ActiveX and WebObjects are among the raft of features available for a Web site that aims to stand above the crowd.

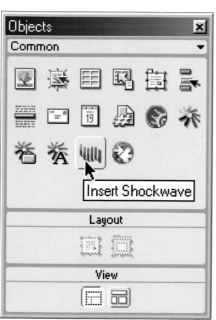

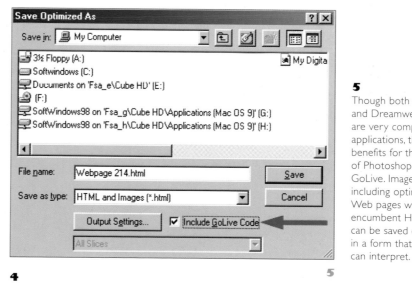

5
Though both GoLive and Dreamweaver are very competent applications, there are benefits for the user of Photoshop in using GoLive. Images, including optimized Web pages with their encumbent HTML, can be saved directly in a form that GoLive can interpret.

4
A range of resources (including the aforementioned Flash and ShockWave) can be placed on the page using the Dreamweaver toolbox.

4

5

ASSEMBLING SITES

Most Web sites are constructed from a range of different components; these are generally called the "Web assets." They might include animations, movies, graphics, text, illustrations, and sets of buttons that together form the navigation system for the Web sites. As we have already seen, most of these assets are created using different software packages. This is one of the reasons why the Web designer's job can be so difficult. The one individual needs to have a good understand of a range of different content types and the technology used to create them. In small production companies the same person might need to be proficient in a range of software packages necessary to control and produce assets, from fields as varied as 3D rendering, movie making, and 2D graphics.

The first part of the Web design process is the planning phase. It is here that the general concept for the site is first documented. The content is laid out and divided into its different asset categories. Specifications for the production of each of the assets are noted and passed to the individual designer, who will be responsible for creating that particular site component. While the assets are being generated, the overall design of the site is nailed down. It is critical during this part of the process to ensure that good communication exists between those individuals responsible for making the different assets and the head designer, because this will determine how well the various parts fit together.

1 | 2
The latest Web production packages use a WYSIWYG approach to the coordination and layout of Web assets.

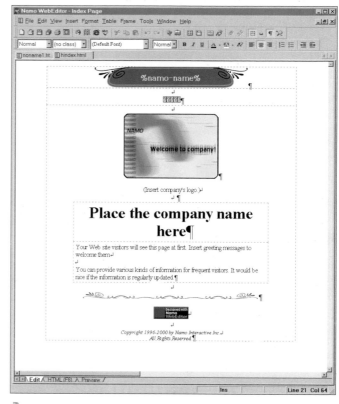

3

Some Web packages use a desktop publishing approach to the organization and placing of Web content. These are particularly suited to designers making the switch from a print background.

3

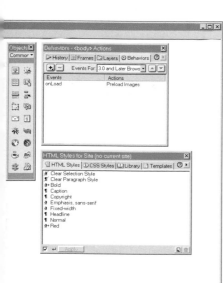

Bringing together all the assets into a single well-organized, well-laid-out, and, most importantly, fully functional Web site occurs within a software package generally referred to as a page layout or Web design program. These packages allow the designer to combine all the major components into one visual form. In the early days of Web work, the programs looked and functioned like basic word processors and designers needed to have a comprehensive understanding of the HTML language to be able to construct sites. Thankfully the software manufacturing companies now provide us with Web layout tools, which are WYSIWYG (what you see is what you get). That is, designers can now lay out the components of pages in much the same fashion as they do when creating layout spreads for a magazine using page layout software.

THE PROCESS 1

Planning: Planning is the first stage of creating any website. Traditionally this stage involves drafting the specifications, performance guidelines, and content lists of the site. This information is usually documented and combined into a single document called the Design Specification. This formal approach, though still a major component of information-driven site production, has largely been replaced by a more interactive approach to Web design that involves the prototyping of design ideas in the planning stages of production.

Essentially this means that a working model of the site's hierarchy containing main pages and details of content is generated in the planning stages. The latest releases of software programs like Adobe's GoLive now contain features specifically created to manage this approach to Web design. Using such tools the designer can put together a visual model that can be trialled in consultations with the client. The model should be tested thoroughly because any problems with the site architecture will be much harder to fix at a later stage.

120

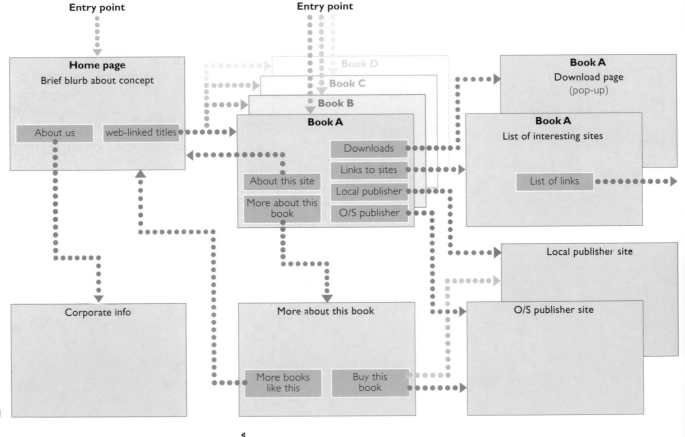

If you are planning on developing anything other than the most simple website, it is essential to begin by mapping out the links between the various pages within the site. This need not be a high-tech operation—a pencil and a piece of paper is ideal.

2
The page-layout program brings together the many assets of the website.

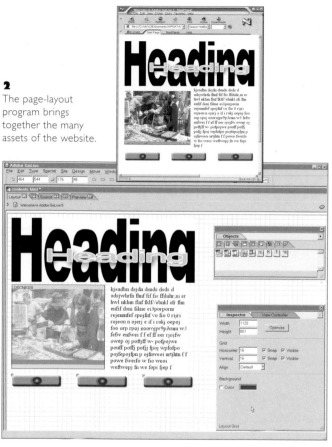

3
Some programs contain a design or prototyping module that allows a visual representation of the website, and its many pages, to be constructed and used to help clarify design requirements.

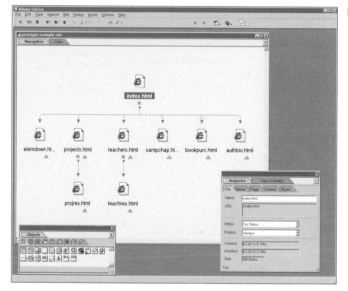

Creating assets: With the major components of the Web design decided in the planning stages, now comes the task of creating the site's assets. Depending on the nature of the site being constructed, this may involve a variety of producers using different software packages to create a range of Web components. Good communication through this phase of the project will help to ensure that all components meet the requirements of the design specification. For this reason it is important to ensure that issues such as file size, color palettes, and browser and bandwidth restrictions are clearly laid out and taken into account by all content producers.

Bringing the components together: As all the components are completed, the website is put together in a production package. In some cases the prototype design generated in the planning stages can be used as a base for the full production site. In this phase the skills of graphic designer and computer technician are combined to produce a site that is both visually stimulating and technically practical. Modern Web production packages takes much of the complex and frustrating work out of this process. Generally these pieces of software take a visual approach to the construction of pages and, to a large degree, work in a similar fashion to print-based page layout programs.

THE PROCESS 2

Testing phase: The importance of this phase cannot be overstated. It is here that the results of the planning, asset creation, and assembly stages are assessed and, if need be, adjusted. The testing process is made easier because most modern site-construction programs contain built-in testing features. Most are able to emulate different working platforms and contain preview features that show the site in a variety of browsers. In addition to this type of local testing, it is critical that a draft version of the site be placed on the net so that factors like download time are not just estimated, but are based in reality.

Going live: The last stage in the process is to release the final site to the public. In doing so it is important to realize that just because you have created a great site does not mean that people will automatically know that it is there, or will want to visit it. It is just as important to advertise and draw attention to a new website, as it is to publicize other information products. Saving specific metatags that describe the contents of your site in the heading section of your pages will help Web search engines provide discriminating information about your site.

The sheer number of files associated with any sizeable Web project makes tracking the different assets a difficult process. As part of the planning stage it is important to establish a common approach to the storage of all of the project's components or assets. This means that a common naming standard needs to be set up and used across the whole of the project. As some servers still are restricted to using an "eight character—period—three character" naming system,

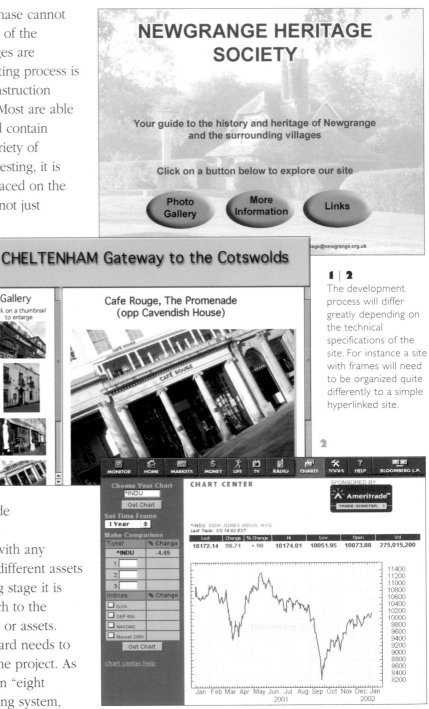

1 | 2
The development process will differ greatly depending on the technical specifications of the site. For instance a site with frames will need to be organized quite differently to a simple hyperlinked site.

this might be a good base-level specification used for naming all asset files. Along with naming standards, it is also important to establish a hierarchy of folders, or directories, used to store assets, both when they are uploaded to the Web and when they are housed locally. Being clear about where specific files should be stored makes the production process quicker and any revision process performed on the site at a later date more efficient.

It is very tempting for new designers, or designers who are used to working by themselves, to skip over the job of setting down the specifications for a website project. After all, isn't it more important to have the site up and running rather than spending time writing down the specifications? This attitude is essentially short-term thinking and will lead to a less efficient process and in

the longer run, more time spent putting together complex sites.

The general rule of thumb used to divide the assets of a Web project is based on the types of files, or file formats, associated with each asset's contents. For instance, movie files, animations files and still images are usually separated into different folders and directories. Alternatively, if there are two different versions of the site, one that is HTML based and one that uses Flash, then it would make sense to divide the assets for each of these sites into folders/directories titled Flash and HTML. Under these parent directories there might still be folders/directories that separate the files based on their asset type, but because there are essentially two different sites sitting together, dividing the assets in this manner is more logical.

123

3

A site incorporating advanced graphics, advertising, and forms may require a whole team of specialists to develop and maintain it.

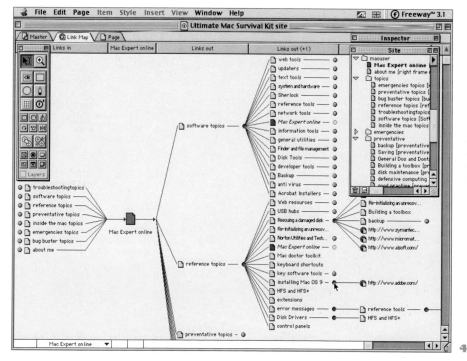

4

Mapping the links from a page can be tedious business, but with complex sites it can be vital to keep track of your overall site navigation structure. Look for site- and link-mapping features in your Web design tool in order to keep on top of this when handling large projects.

4

DESIGN FOR ALL ... OR JUST A FEW

One of the biggest problems facing Web designers is the fact that the machines used to view the pages you create cannot be the same for every member of your audience. Most people understand that it is necessary to ensure that the pages that you create are able to be viewed on Macintosh, Windows, and UNIX computers, but there is also the added complication of several different types of browsers, each with several versions. Each of these factors can cause changes in the way that pages are viewed. With this in mind, the major software manufacturers have added preview features into the programs. With the latest releases, it is possible to preview your Web pages not only in different versions of a specific browser, but also in different browsers. An extra feature of some packages allows the designer to simulate the environment of a different computer platform right from their desktop.

Because of the sheer number of possible configurations, it is critical that a substantial amount of time in the production process of a major project is allocated to testing on a range of platforms and in a range of browsers. A good testing phase can save a lot of reworking later on.

When you are designing for the Web, you must be aware about the makeup of your target audience. If you are trying to create a Web site that can be viewed by the widest possible audience, then it is very important that you design the site so that it can be displayed on as

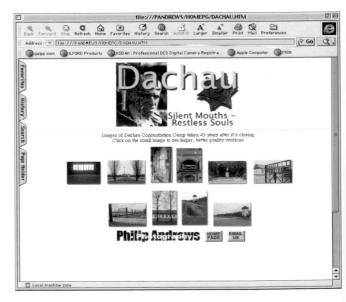

1 | 2 | 3
The testing phase should include previewing the Web pages in as many different types of browsers as possible.

124

4

5

4 | 5
Sometimes even HTML-coded resources will look different in alternative browsers. Though structurally identical, and viewed on the same platform, even an innocuous page such as this one from Amazon takes on a different look when viewed in Netscape Navigator (left), compared with Internet Explorer (right).

6

many machines and browsers as possible. This will preclude the use of all advanced and plug-in-based technologies. If a viewer needs to install a third-party plug-in to see your pages, then often he or she would choose to go to a competitor's site if it is more readily available. The challenge for designers, when creating pages for a mass audience, is producing a creative and well-laid-out site while using only a basic set of features.

Alternatively, if your audience is prepared to embrace the latest technology for the sake of a visually rich, dynamic, and exciting Web experience, then you will be in a position where you can use some cutting-edge features in your design.

7

6 | 7 | 8
This page from BBCi takes particular care not to disenfranchise visitors without plug-ins. Those whose browsers support RealPlayer can watch a replay of the latest "60seconds" news program. Those without are directed to the more prosaic (but equally informative) text page.

8

INFORMATION AND DESIGN-BASED SITES

Aquick scan of the Internet will show a range of solutions that designers have used to present information to their target audience. You should immediately notice that there are at least two distinct types of Web page design—there are those sites whose primary function is to present as much information as succinctly as possible, and those sites whose role is to provide a rich interactive experience.

Different design approaches are necessary for the production of these two, very different, types of sites. The major software packages tend to align themselves with either one of these approaches. Some provide

3

London College of Fashion
Prospectus 2001

THE LONDON INSTITUTE

1

The Internet Encyclopedia of Philosophy

The Chinese Room Argument

The Chinese room argument - John Searle's (1980a) thought experiment and associated (1984) derivation - is one of the best known and widely credited counters to claims of artificial intelligence (AI), i.e., to claims that computers *do* or at least *can* (someday might) think. According to Searle's original presentation, the argument is based on two truths: *brains cause minds*, and *syntax doesn't suffice for semantics*. Its target, Searle dubs "strong AI": "according to strong AI," according to Searle, "the computer is not merely a tool in the study of the mind, rather the appropriately programmed computer really *is* a mind in the sense that computers given the right programs can be literally said to *understand* and have other cognitive states" (1980a, p. 417). Searle contrasts "strong AI" to "weak AI". According to weak AI, according to Searle, computers just *simulate* thought, their seeming understanding isn't real (just as-if) understanding, their seeming calculation as-if calculation, etc.; nevertheless, computer simulation is useful for *studying* the mind (as for studying the weather and other things).

2

News
Weather
Horoscopes
E-mail

infoplease.com
all the knowledge you need

Almanacs
Dictionary
Encyclopedia
Atlas

search [ ] in [All Infoplease ▾] (go!)

Home
Daily Almanac
Back to School 🎒

World
United States
History & Gov't
Biography
Sports
Entertainment
Business
Society & Culture
Health & Science
Weather

Homework Center
Fact Monster

Search Biographies
[ ] (go!)

Sources:
Atlas
Almanacs
Encyclopedia
Dictionary

E-mail this page

HotWords
Highlight any

This Day in History

s e p t e m b e r   1

1807
Former U. S. Vice President Aaron Burr was found innocent of treason.

1923
A devastating earthquake struck the Japanese cities of Tokyo and Yokohama. Nearly 150,000 people were killed and over two million were left homeless.

1939
World War II began when Nazi Germany invaded Poland

1983
A Korean Air Lines Boeing 747 was shot down by a Soviet jet fighter, killing all 269 people aboard.

1985
A joint U. S. - French expedition located the wreck of the *Titanic* 560 miles off the coast of Newfoundland.

Yesterday | Tomorrow
or choose another day:
[Jan ▾] [ ] Go!

1 | 2
There are many contrasting views about what the Web should be used for and how content should be conveyed. The designers of The Internet Encyclopedia of Philosophy (www.utm.edu/ research/iep) and infoplease.com are believers in keeping the Web firmly rooted in functionality.

Fashion Space

4

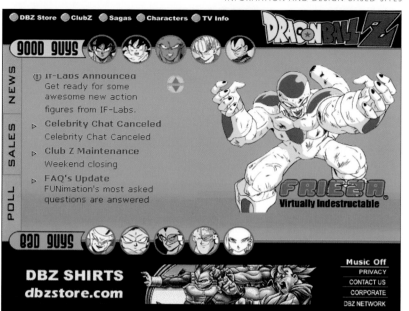

5

built-in features, such as live linking to back-end database files, that ensure that their product is well suited for the production of information sites. Other manufacturers provide a highly visual work environment that suits the production of design-orientated sites.

The big names, like Macromedia's Dreamweaver and Adobe's GoLive, are still at the forefront of the field. They both provide a level of sophistication and comprehensive features that make them difficult to compete with. This does not mean that there are not other good packages on the market. In fact, it would pay for new designers to look at the range of options available before settling on a package that suits the way they work.

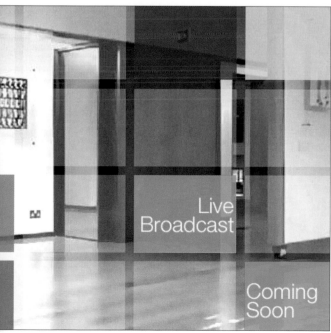

3 | 4 | 5
The designers of the London College of Fashion site (www. linst.ac.uk) and at the kids' game site Dragonball Z (www. dragonballz.com) want the Web to be as visually rich and engaging as possible. What matters most for any site is that it adheres to certain elementary design principles and is suited to the content and the needs of its audience. In this respect, all these sites on these pages are well designed.

USING TEMPLATES AND WIZARDS

Unless you are a full-time Web designer, then the prospect of having to master a range of different content software packages, as well as a Web-layout package, can seem very daunting. For this reason several of the software manufacturers provide simple step-by-step guides to making basic Web pages and sites. Although at first you might be concerned that by using one of these wizards your sites will appear very similar to other sites created with the same package, there are usually enough variables to help ensure different results.

The advantage of working in this way is that some of the steep learning curve associated with putting together functional and practical Web sites is alleviated. The program takes care of the underlying complexities of

tasks such as writing the code for rollover buttons, or embedding a third-party plug-in that will display a movie file. Using these guides, the designer can concentrate on the layout of page elements rather than concerns such as the correct syntax of HTML code.

Starting the production process with a template can also speed up the production process of Web sites. Unlike word processing, the templates for Web design might not determine the look of the pages, but rather how those pages function. For instance, capturing data from a Web form can be a complex matter. A form template can contain the background code used to capture, sort, and present the information entered by a visitor to your site. The designer maintains control over variables that determine how the form looks to the user, but the template provides the complex coding that is needed to make the form function.

128

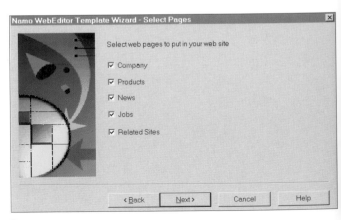

1
Namo WebEditor is typical in its approach to generating template pages from bare-bones information. First, choose the overall visual style and layout for your site.

2
There may be a subset of template types for your selection. In this instance, you can choose between a Company or a Personal Web site.

3
Having chosen Company, for instance, you can put a tick next to each additional template page suggested by the wizard. This will produce a simple multipage site instead of just one page.

Of course, in a professional context this only works if you are prepared to put in the work to customize the appearance of the pages still further. The big disadvantage of using templates is that other people like you are using them for their sites, too. The last thing you want for a professional or commercial project is to end up with a site that looks precisely like someone else's, except for different button graphics. Use templates and wizards with care.

Also, don't take it for granted that professional Web-page layout software comes with perfectly designed templates. Usually the only difference between the templates found in a consumer home-page program and a full site-design and development package is the quality of the HTML; possibly the cheaper templates will look a little uglier, but not much. Ultimately, the quality of the visual design is in your hands.

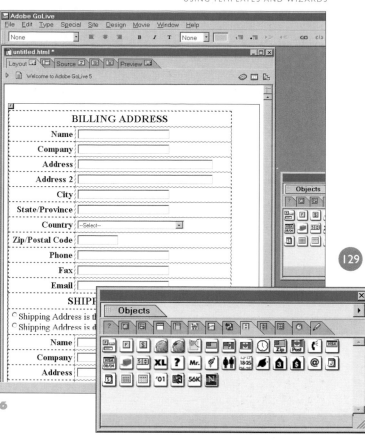

6

4

Finish off by entering in your custom details, such as company name, contact information, and so on. The wizard will insert them into appropriate pages and locations in the site template.

5

And here's the result. It may not be pretty, but you have a clutch of pages ready for quick customization. It's easier to stamp your personality on a template like this than get bogged down with "artist's block."

6 | 7

Using templates as a base for your design can save you from having to wrestle with complex HTML code that drives site features such as sophisticated forms.

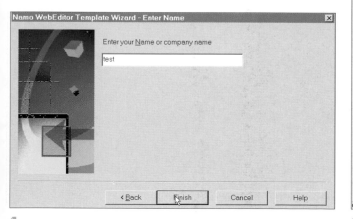

4

7

5

ONLINE IMAGE PORTFOLIOS

As we have seen, the speed with which a Web page is presented is determined by the size of the file and the bandwidth of the Net connection. Good Web design achieves a balance of file size and asset quality. As well as compression technologies to reduce the size of large files, download speed can be increased when careful thought is given to the way that information is stored and presented in the site. A good example of this reorganization of information to cater for Web use are the gallery pages of many photography and art sites. For the artist it is important to show the original works of art as large, and with as much quality, as possible. But size and quality, when combined, usually mean that the image files will be large and very slow to download. The problems are magnified because, generally, artists also want to display several images of their work in one place to simulate an exhibition space. The more image files included on the page, the longer it will take to download.

In practical terms, the prospective audience will need a lot of patience to view a gallery full of images. The solution to this quandary is to create a front page full of small thumbnail versions of the artwork. The thumbnails use smaller dimensions and contain less detail than the larger images. This difference means that each of the images has a very small file size. The thumbnail page provides a fast-downloading overview of all the images.

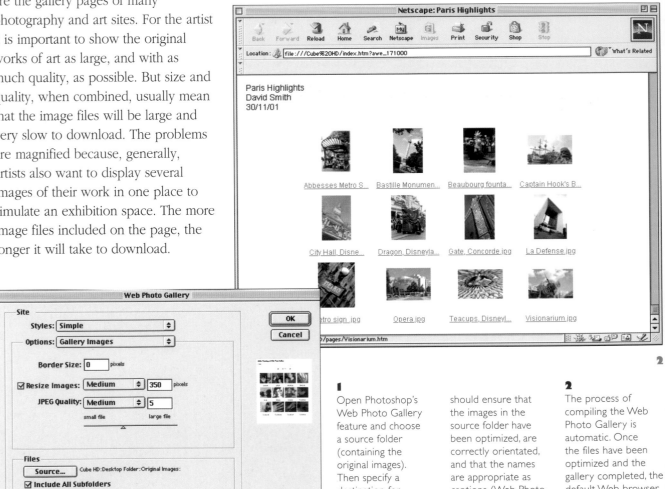

1
Open Photoshop's Web Photo Gallery feature and choose a source folder (containing the original images). Then specify a destination for the Web page components. You should ensure that the images in the source folder have been optimized, are correctly orientated, and that the names are appropriate as captions (Web Photo Gallery uses the file names as captions).

2
The process of compiling the Web Photo Gallery is automatic. Once the files have been optimized and the gallery completed, the default Web browser will open and display the results.

130

From here, the viewer can click on one of the small images and be taken to a special, dedicated page that contains a higher resolution and more detailed version of the same picture. This may seem second nature to us now, but it provides a good example of how changing the way that information is presented can help to provide a creative solution to the file size/bandwidth problems associated with Web delivery of content.

In fact, the creation of an online portfolio comprising a front page of thumbnails and a gallery of higher-resolution images (which can be viewed in turn by selecting the respective thumbnail) can be achieved using many image-manipulation applications. Here we have created a simple portfolio using a small folder of images and Photoshop. Other than providing necessary information, the process—including the generation of the required HTML—is totally automatic.

In creating an online portfolio, Photoshop can make its own judgment on the image size and compression required. This is often a good "first guess," but as originator of the site you may want to refine these settings somewhat.

Look out, too, for applications that can produce Web slide shows. Slide shows provide a useful adjunct to (rather than replacement for) the standard portfolio, offering a sequenced display of your finest images without the need for intercession by the viewer. You can rely on their innate passive nature to allow your images to drift by them!

131

3
Though the gallery is still "local," it will function in exactly the same way as it would when uploaded to a Web site. Click on a thumbnail and the corresponding image will open.

4
Photoshop offers a limited number of templates for the gallery. This version displays the image thumbnails in a scalable, navigable bar across the base of the window.

STREAMING CONTENT

Streaming Web content allows the initial section of a video or audio file to be viewed or heard while the rest the content is still being delivered. Used extensively for Web video, complex Flash sites, and 3D animation, streaming is a way around the problem of delivering high-quality Net content through low bandwidth connections. Software packages used to enhance and edit this type of content often include features designed specifically for optimizing files so that they can be streamed on viewer's browsers.

Video and audio plug-ins and viewers, such as RealAudio, QuickTime, and Microsoft's Windows Media Player, all contain the ability to handle streaming Web content. As bandwidth continues to increase, so too will the overall quality of streaming media that is available for Internet delivery. Already major television, radio, and music companies provide streaming audiovisual experiences throughout the world. Web surfers can switch between listening to music from the Top 10, seeing a trailer for a new movie, and catching up on the latest international news by clicking from one streaming channel to another.

132

1
Windows Media Player is one of the major streaming video viewers that is available on the market.

2
RealPlayer, like Media Player and QuickTime, provides the ability to view a streamed Web-delivered video right on your desktop.

3
The QuickTime viewer provides panorama viewing features, as well as those used to view streamed video.

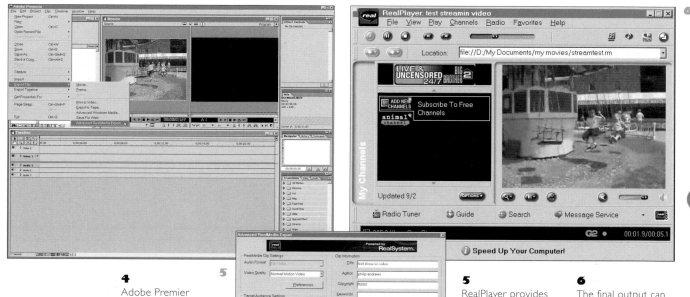

4

Adobe Premier provides users with the option to optimize their video output so that it suits Web delivery.

5

RealPlayer provides the optimization plug-in for the Adobe product, allowing users to match the quality of the video product with the connection speed of the audience.

6

The final output can then be delivered and shown using the RealPlayer viewer.

9

Bloomberg's streaming video on QuickTime is slightly different, in that it is a 24-hour feed from the company's existing satellite and cable broadcast channels. There are no introductions or summaries: it's live TV in real time.

7 | 8

CNN Headline News and the Weather Channel both offer free streaming video through QuickTime. These are specially produced movies, which are updated throughout the day, so that a visitor can return in a few hours to find that the movies have been changed.

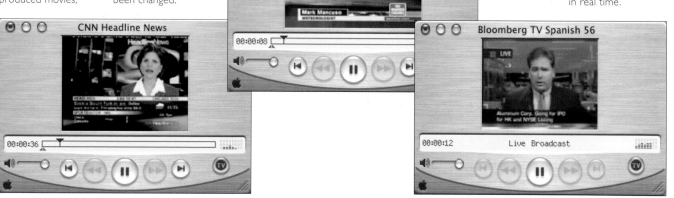

DESIGN AND NAVIGATION CONSISTENCY

A lot of Web design is based on providing a consistent look and feel to a site so that, as viewers move from one page to another, they have a general understanding of "where they are and where they are going." This means that the navigation system has to have a consistent approach to moving between pages and sections of the site. Because many sites use visual metaphors as the basis for the design of pages, consistency is not just about making sure that navigation buttons are positioned in the same place on each page, but should also take into account the thematic and esthetic ideas that underpin the system. For instance, if the pages have a jungle feel, then it might be appropriate to use animal icons for buttons in the navigation section of the site. If at a different part of the site the animal icon buttons are changed to geometric arrows and stylized words, then viewers are apt to lose their way.

Apart from the thematic concerns, the structure and sequencing of pages also need to be consistent. Viewers need to be aware of exactly where they are within the site at all times. They also need to be able to

134

1

A site map provides your visitors with a quick overview in case they get lost. Note how watch manufacturer G-Shock uses a watch-style interface for its pages, which is maintained throughout the site.

2 | 3

It is important when developing the visual approach to be used in a site that the design is consistent throughout all pages, buttons, and imagery.

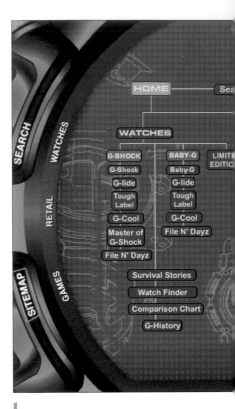
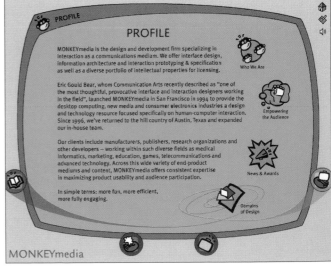

1

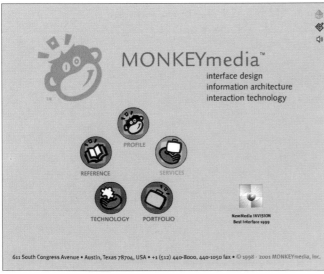

2

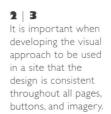

3

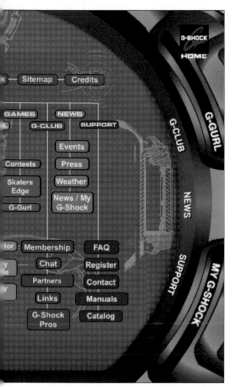

move to any part of the site with very few button clicks. To help with this, designers often provide a site map as a reference to the major sections and pages contained within a Web space. This overview allows the members of the audience to get a good mental picture of how the site is constructed and how best to find the information they need.

In addition to a site map, a lot of Web sites contain search buttons. This feature can cut down on the amount of time needed to locate specific information within a large, or complex, group of pages. It is important that the design, navigation, and sequencing of pages within a Web site provide information in away that is as intuitive as possible. If at any stage the user feels lost when trying move around a Web site, then the designer has failed in this task. The aim is for all such design to be as transparent as possible. The navigation system and the information design of your site should show the viewer "what you've got, and how to get there, and then get out of the way!"

4 | 5
The Roald Dahl site uses a combination of very consistent styling, Flash animation, and Quentin Blake's familiar artwork to ensure that even young children can navigate their way through.

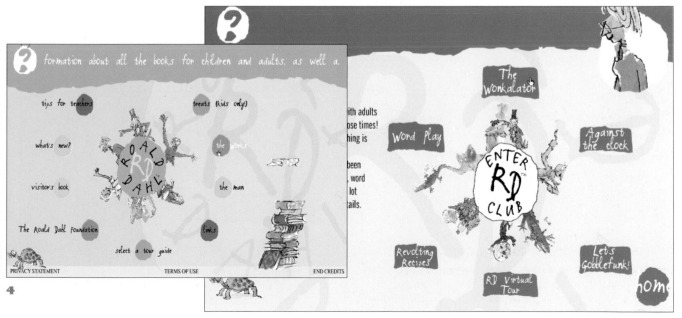

4

5

A FINAL WORD ON DESIGN

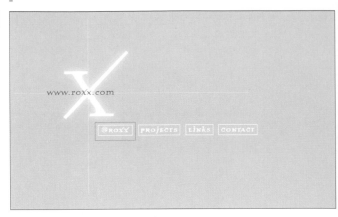

AFRICAN VOICES

HISTORY

Follow the timeline as it guides you through the millennia of Africa's history. Your journey begins with the origins of humankind and ends with current challenges. Learn how Africans have developed cities and empires, philosophies and religions, technology and trade. Like all people tackling life's challenges, Africans have met with failure and success, tragedy and triumph.

Humans Arise   Nile Valley   Mali   Africans in Spain

MAIN   HISTORY   THE

Avoid the overused. It can be tempting when creating your first Web site to follow the lead of many designers before you, by constructing a site that looks and feels like many you have seen before. This approach will have the advantage of providing design solutions quickly, but the end product will fail to stand apart from all the other sites on the Internet. Web design is still a comparatively new field, and new designers should take up the exciting challenge of producing Web sites in a way that has not been seen before.

Know your audience. As we have already seen, the nature of the audience who uses your Web products determines the sophistication of the technology you can use, as well as the complexity of the content you can include. Having a good understanding of the audience you are trying to reach will help you discern the level of features, and the type of design, that can form the basis for your site.

Make it simple. The old design adage of "keeping it simple" applies as much in the Web world as it does in other forms of design. Visitors to your site should be able to access with ease the information and ideas contained within the site. Overly complex and fussy design can make this task more difficult.

A good site is a fast site. This skill of the Web designer is being able to balance the requirements of good design with the limitations of Web delivery. Always keep in mind that a fantastic site that runs well on a local machine will only be a success if it functions just as well when delivered by limited bandwidth. Compression techniques combined with good information design will help to keep files small and thus increase delivery speed.

Keep your pages browser-neutral. Don't make the mistake of believing there is only one browser that your audience will use to view your work. At the moment there are still several different types of browsers on the

1 | 2
Good design does not have to be complex. Simple sites often provide an elegant solution to Web delivery and presence.

3
The very best examples of Web design adhere to age-old design principles. Harmony of color and texture, expert use of space, and carefully considered typography are all evident.

136

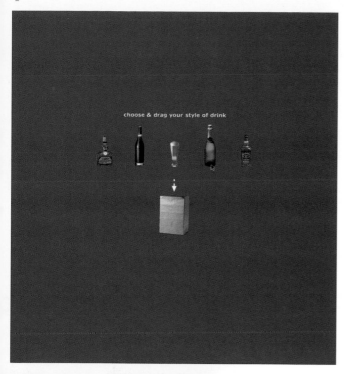

choose & drag your style of drink

market. Each of these programs is likely to display your pages in a slightly different way. A good designer will be aware of the differences between each of the browsing systems and will make allowances in his or her design to accommodate these differences.

Test, test, and test again. The role of good testing cannot be overstated in the production of quality Web sites. Apart from checking to see that all the features, links, and buttons within the production are functioning correctly, testing can also highlight problems associated with differences in browsers, browser versions, and computer platforms.

Good luck!

137

4
The human mind was wired to respond to images long before text was invented, so make use of them. By keeping images small and neat, not only does the site look cool and uncluttered, but the speed at which it works will be improved.

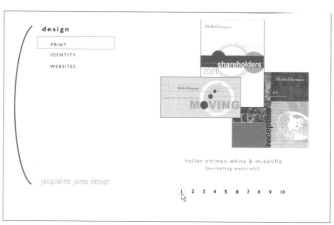

5

5 | 6
A fast site is a good site. Making your audience wait for complex imagery to download is a good way to turn them off. Making use of large areas of white or plain colored text is not only good design but also speeds up delivery.

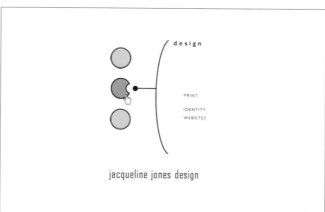

6

LONELY PLANET

Though www.lonelyplanet.com is not a site rich in photographic imagery, the designers have made very effective use of a range of graphic and vector images in its navigation and design style. In it, they pay special attention to the use of symbols and metaphors to create an easy-to-navigate site.

The site is peppered with simple, yet highly effective image maps linking viewers to associated pages or links to other interesting locations. As a leader in the travel industry, the Lonely Planet site is a shining example of great design and quality graphics.

2

1 | 2

This is the entry page for www.lonelyplanet.com. The page is packed with beautifully clear graphics. Interestingly, to avoid that feeling of "I've been here before…," some of the graphics change with each new page view. The symbols and graphics are easy to comprehend, while remaining hip and upbeat. For example, to get to its "On the Road" section, the designer has used a variation on the typical international road sign—complete with the obligatory bullet holes added by a passing redneck. Nice touch.

1

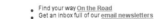

lonely planet online

CALL WAITING, CALL HOME, CALL OF THE WILD.

what's on your planet this week
25 July, Pipesmoking World Championship, Vorupøor, Denmark
C'mon baby, light my fire: it's Europe's slowest drag race

search

worldguide

theme guides

the thorn tree

the scoop

eKno

on the road

postcards

propaganda

health

subWWWay

talk 2 us
feedback

??? FAQ

Destination Nigeria
Nigeria's female parliamentarians are threatening to parade topless in protest at the 'unwarranted evil' visited on women politicians in the country: it's business as usual for West Africa's simmering political and cultural hotspot. Get the naked truth on the home of juju, efo and Durbar.

- Find your way On the Road
- Get an inbox full of our email newsletters

Scoop: Boiling Point
While the eyes of the world are on Genoa, Etna's been throwing more tantrums in Sicily, Argentinians are have had it up to here with austerity measures, the US State Department advises paranoia in the Middle East, Galapagos sea lions are culled for vanity's sake, Russians plan a literary theme park, Christian clerics favor abstinence in Kenya's AIDS fight, and Basque terrorism escalates.

 Get a Lonely Planet guidebook

or Upgrade one here

Plug-in to July & August
Check out Beck in Paris, Madonna in New York or the the Boston Pops in Tokyo. Just three of the 1,793 things to do in the July - August editions of **CitySync What's On.**

Lonely Planet spouts better Propaganda
Lonely Planet announces the relaunch of its online catalogue & shop, Propaganda. The new Propaganda has been designed to brainwash you into buying things with its easy-to-use shopping basket & search tools. Browse our shop to find guidebooks or great reads like *Black on Black*, which has just been shortlisted for a major award.

Special Offer: City Packs
City guide plus restaurant guide
Planning a trip to London, Melbourne, Sydney or San Francisco? Lonely Planet has made planning a great time in these cities even easier. For a limited time, you can buy the city guide and restaurant guide together in one great City Pack.

Join eKno - get $5
Earn a $5 bonus for joining eKno, Lonely Planet's all-in-one travel communications service. Talk is cheap and so are you - just pre-charge your calls and get ready to gab.

eKno number [＿＿] PIN [＿＿] [login]

Ticket to ride
Must...stop...clicking....

BLAH! Shoot your mouth off
Party at my place!

You want newsletters? Oh, we got newsletters. Sign up here and see.

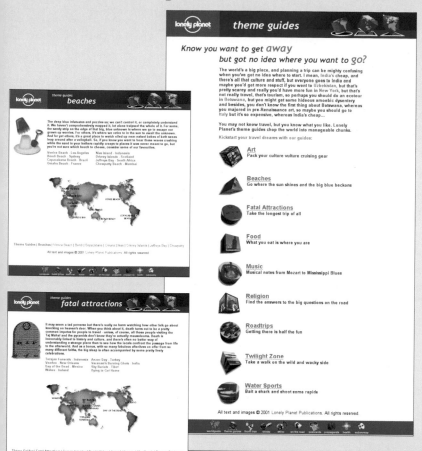

theme guides

Know you want to get *away*
but got no idea where you want to *go?*

The world's a big place, and planning a trip can be mighty confusing when you've got no idea where to start. I mean, India's cheap, and there's all that culture and stuff, but everyone goes to India and maybe you'd get more respect if you went to Uzbekistan, but that's pretty scary and really you'd have more fun in New York, but that's not really travel, that's tourism, so perhaps you should do an ecotour in Botswana, but you might get some hideous amoebic dysentery and besides, you don't know the first thing about Botswana, whereas you majored in pre-Renaissance art, so maybe you should go to Italy but it's so expensive, whereas India's cheap...

You may not know travel, but you know what you like. Lonely Planet's theme guides chop the world into manageable chunks.

Kickstart your travel dreams with our guides:

Art
Pack your culture vulture cruising gear

Beaches
Go where the sun shines and the big blue beckons

Fatal Attractions
Take the longest trip of all

Food
What you eat is where you are

Music
Musical notes from Mozart to Mississippi Blues

Religion
Find the answers to the big questions on the road

Roadtrips
Getting there is half the fun

Twilight Zone
Take a walk on the wild and wacky side

Water Sports
Bait a shark and shoot some rapids

All text and images © 2001 Lonely Planet Publications. All rights reserved.

3 | 4 | 5 | 6 | 7

Lonelyplanet.com offers an array of offbeat sections within its site (3). These include: the ultimate in beaches from around the world (4) and great places to experience deathly rituals in all their funereal glory (5).

Postcards offers feedback from travelers on the road (6), while clicking on the Band-Aid symbol whisks those with travel paranoia to cures for Delhi-belly and tips on sharing your hotel room with a range of insects (7).

theme guides
beaches

The deep blue infatuates and puzzles us; we can't control it, or completely understand it. We haven't comprehensively mapped it, let alone traipsed the whole of it. For some, the sandy strip on the edge of that big, blue unknown is where we go to escape our grown-up worries. For others, it's where we retire to in the sun to await the unknown. And for yet others, it's a great place to watch oiled up near-naked babes of both sexes leap around after a volleyball. So, if you know you want to hear those waves crashing while the sand in your bathers rapidly creeps to places it was never meant to go, but you're not sure which beach to choose, consider some of our favourites.

Venice Beach - Los Angeles
Bondi Beach - Sydney
Copacabana Beach - Brazil
Omaha Beach - France

Nias Island - Indonesia
Orkney Islands - Scotland
Jeffreys Bay - South Africa
Chowpatty Beach - Mumbai

Theme Guides | Beaches | Venice Beach | Bondi | Copacabana | Omaha | Nias | Orkney Islands | Jeffreys Bay | Chowpatty

All text and images © 2001 Lonely Planet Publications. All rights reserved.

HEALTH
Pills, ills and bellyaches

Who can appreciate the joys of exploring exotic locations when you'd sell your grandmother for directions to the nearest toilet?

Successful travelling is healthy travelling. All it takes is a bit of planning, eating carefully while you're away, and recognising the early warning signs of possible health-care disasters. The list of potential ailments described below looks daunting, but a little knowledge of basic precautions - and a little luck - can ensure that you experience little more hardship than jetlag, upset stomach, too much duty-free bevvy, blisters

predeparture planning | keeping healthy | women's health | diseases and ailments | health links

worldguide | eKno | on the road | thorn tree | postcards | propaganda | health | subWWWay | scoop | feedback

lonely planet

Text & maps © Lonely Planet 2001

theme guides
fatal attractions

It may seem a tad perverse but there's really no harm watching how other folk go about knocking on heaven's door. When you think about it, death turns out to be a pretty common impetus for people to travel - unless, of course, all those people visiting the Taj Mahal and the pyramids don't know they're actually mausoleums. Death is inexorably linked to history and culture, and there's often no better way of understanding a strange place than to see how the locals confront the passage from life to the afterworld. And as a bonus, with so many fabulous afterlives on offer from so many different faiths, the big sleep is often accompanied by some pretty lively celebrations.

Torajan Funerals - Indonesia
Voodoo - New Orleans
Day of the Dead - Mexico
Wakes - Ireland

Anzac Day - Turkey
Varanasi's Burning Ghats - India
Sky Burials - Tibet
Dying to Get Home

Theme Guides | Fatal Attractions | Torajan | Voodoo | Dead | Wakes | Anzac | Varanasi | Sky Burials | Dying to Get Home

All text and images © 2001 Lonely Planet Publications. All rights reserved.

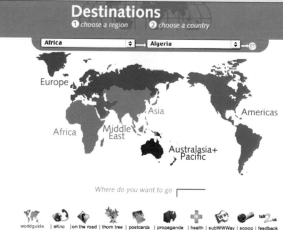

Destinations
❶ *choose a region* ❷ *choose a country*

Africa | Algeria → Go

Europe

Asia

Africa

Middle East

Australasia + Pacific

Americas

Where do you want to go

worldguide | eKno | on the road | thorn tree | postcards | propaganda | health | subWWWay | scoop | feedback

lonely planet
home

Text & maps © Lonely Planet 2001

post **cards**

If you don't buy into brochure blurbs, you'll know that fellow travellers can be one of the best sources of info around. We get a mountain of mail from travellers on the road, covering everything from how to get a summer job in Guatemala to how to find a cold beer in Timbuktu. We want to share this stuff with other travellers atsap so we haven't checked the facts they contain. The letters make great reading, but be smart and treat tips with caution until you suss things out for yourself.

Talk 2 us

worldguide | eKno | on the road | thorn tree | postcards | propaganda | health | subWWWay | scoop | feedback

lonely planet
home

Text & maps © Lonely Planet 2001

Destinations
Middle East

Destinations
Europe

8 | 9 | 10

For quick access to travel information, visitors click on the world map to zoom in on specific areas for detailed destination-related information.

2WIST

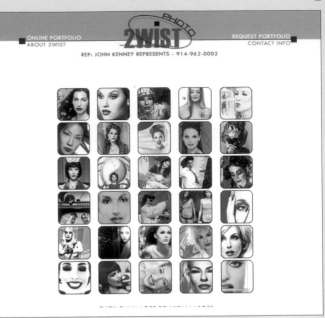

Ond of those pleasant little discoveries, www.2wist.com features the creative output of photographer Ken Pivak and Photoshop maestro Suzette Troche. The site is exceptional in that there is almost no text or copy—just page after page of high-quality photography and accomplished digital imaging.

Navigation is the way it should be—a no-brainer. Click on an image to see it enlarged, click an arrow to move forward and backward through the portfolio sections. Impressive, visual, and at times almost surreal imagery wrapped into a very user-friendly site.

3

ONLINE PORTFOLIO
ABOUT 2WIST

REQUEST PORTFOLIO
CONTACT INFO

REP: JOHN KENNEY REPRESENTS - 914-962-0002

Welcome to the world of 2wist Photo...

Thanks for stopping by.
This site is best viewed at 1024x768

Please feel free to drop us a l

Click here for the latest 2wist news...

Need some photoshop adv

All images on this website are @2001 2wist Photo

2 | 3 | 4 | 5
Navigation is simple throughout. Click a photo and view the impressive photography behind each campaign or assignment. Clicking the left or right arrows quickly takes you through the portfolio sections.

4

143

ONLINE PORTFOLIO
ABOUT 2WIST

REQUEST PORTFOLIO
CONTACT INFO

REP: JOHN KENNEY REPRESENTS - 914-962-0002

ONLINE PORTFOLIO

Spec Ad For English Ideas

▶

oto and may not be reproduced without permission.

ONLINE PORTFOLIO
ABOUT 2WIST

REQUEST PORTFOLIO
CONTACT INFO

REP: JOHN KENNEY REPRESENTS - 914-962-0002

ONLINE PORTFOLIO

Client: PEI Magazine

◀   ▶

All images on this website are @2001 2wist Photo and may not be reproduced without permission.

1
Clearly lovers of white space, the designers of this innovative and beautiful site have all their luck blowing in the right direction: great photographic imagery and truly superb retouching skills blended with some of the hottest commercial clients any professional imager could ever dream of!

5

AUSTRALIAN INFRONT

A site created by designers, for designers. At the time of publication www.australianinfront.com.au opened with a cute Flash-generated animation and led into a site full of information and downloadable resources on, about, and for designers. InFront is unashamedly Australian in its feel and content, though most of the editorial content points to a wider international audience.

Navigation is relatively easy and the content, as you'd expect, is powerfully design-oriented—most of the images are vector-based. Site contributors enjoy showing off their skills with Web design and animation in a number of unusual ways and formats. There is a degree of interactivity that's fun, but not overwhelming.

1 | 2 | 3 | 4 | 5

While other sites might play with image swaps and small animations to hold the viewer's attention, this site changes its appearance just enough to be disquieting, but not enough to lose a regular visitor's loyalty. Although the Flash intro pictured here will have been superseded by the time you read this, there'll be something else just as neat in its place.

FLASH RESPONSE 02 meets FlashKit's FK01

Flash Response is a project which aims to promote a creative response from one word. For the first time ever, we are accepting entries with external content. That is images not created within the computer and we also have 5 copies of Swift 3d to give away!

BRIEF:
Word: Generate
Your submission must inspire, educate and innovate through the Flash medium.
File size restriction: 400K
Movie Size: 600pixels wide x 250pixels high
Naming convention: yourname.swf (make sure that your entry is 1 self contained swf file)
Use of photography, film, video, scans and audio is permitted.
Deadline: 20th JULY 2001 Send your entries to: infront@australianinfront.com.au

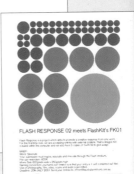

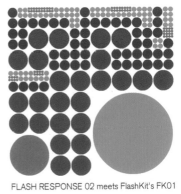

FLASH RESPONSE 02 meets FlashKit's FK01

6 | 7 | 8 | 9 | 10
This site is in
continuous flux, and some
exploration is required to
keep up to date. Even this
can be a roller-coaster
ride of misdirected page
views and confusing
commentary. You might
like it but, at the same
time, you might also hate
the site's often annoying
obscurity. Try it and see
for yourself.

7

8

9

10

CORBIS

O ne of the biggest dealers of images on the planet, Corbis is in the business of selling them as wallpaper, greetings cards, art for corporations, or for the front covers of international publications.

The site www.corbis.com is made up of a simple combination of eye-catching photography and clean vector graphics. The use of text laid over images is particularly strong. Corbis makes good use of pop-up dialog boxes advertising photographic "specials."

As you'd expect from the holder of one of the greatest picture collections on earth, there's no shortage of striking images in this site, although you're never far from the fact that, underlying everything else, this is still predominantly a commerce-driven site.

1 | 2 | 3

146

In many ways the Corbis site is a monument to big business. This company buys entire image archives and vast photographic collections and it is this that enables it to provide customers with a mind-boggling selection of imagery. Unlike most other online image libraries, Corbis deals in royalty-free imagery as well as the more traditional pay-as-you-use licensed images, invoiced for specific applications such as a book cover or company report.

Woman in Man's Lap Playing Slot Machines © Elizabeth Chucker/ZT001012
© 2001 Corbis Corporation. All rights reserved.

4 | 5 | 6 | 7

Break through the beautifully chosen pictures on the Corbis site's opening pages and you soon find yourself down at the business end, with page after page of catalog-style shopping. Select the image for your needs, and just click "Pay."

DEMARCHELIER

Coming from one of the world's top fashion photographers, www.demarchelier.net is packed with images of great beauty and professionalism.

Patrick Demarchelier has photographed some of the most beautiful people alive and presents his studio work (among others) in true photographic form—in the symbolic form of the contact sheet, the starting point for editing a photo shoot.

He has included everything shot on each roll of film—including the chinagraph pen annotations made before printing and a few oddball images shot on location for pure enjoyment.

The luscious monochrome work seems to have lost little in the move to the small screen, presented against a black background for maximum impact. Navigation is aided by pop-out sidebar menus and plenty of subtly highlighted text overlays. A great photographic site.

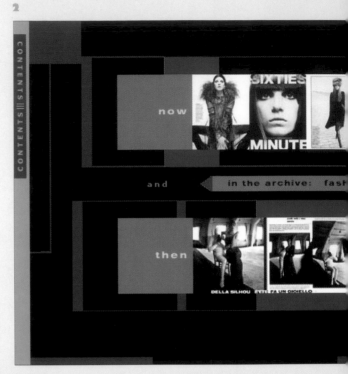

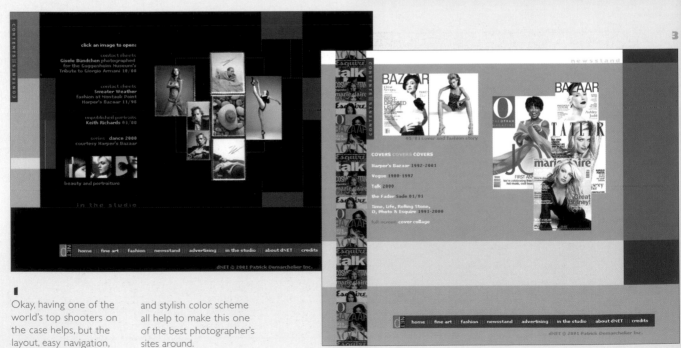

Okay, having one of the world's top shooters on the case helps, but the layout, easy navigation, and stylish color scheme all help to make this one of the best photographer's sites around.

83-2001

2 | 3
Sections are divided into topics like fashion (2) and magazines (3), allowing visitors to shoot straight to the relevant areas for easy viewing.

4 | 5 | 6 | 7
It's plain to see the class that has been injected into this site, right down to the clever use of the photographer's contact sheet as a window into the world of a shoot, stuff-ups and all.

8
Tear sheets assembled for the fashion houses allow the viewer to experience the process, as well as the application, of Demarchelier's work.

advertising

Dior | Louis Vuitton | Celine 99 | Celine 00

Giorgio Armani Acqua di Giò
Giorgio Armani mania

Guerlain Paris Samsara
Guerlain Paris Shalimar

Vauxhall Corsa The New Supermodel

Calvin Klein | Tse | Gap | Estee Lauder

Chanel Coco | Chanel Allure

Karl Lagerfeld Sun Moon Stars

Elizabeth Arden | Carolina Herrera

home ||| fine art ||| fashion ||| newsstand ||| advertising ||| in the studio ||| about dNET ||| credits

dNET © 2001 Patrick Demarchelier Inc.

ELIXIR STUDIO

Marseilles-based Elixir Studios has produced an ingenious mix of eclectic interactive imagery and animated text in this stylish and very offbeat site.

At times unbelievably clever and intricate, www.elixirstudio.com is a Web site that requires time to explore and revisit. Its opening page is host to numerous pop-up virtual reality and interactive animations combining static and moving photo imagery. Navigation, though vicarious at times, follows the almost universal theme of an underground route map to places or locations that seem strangely familiar (although you have almost certainly never visited them).

1 | 2
Elixir is another of those hot/cold Web sites that fascinate and yet frustrate in the same visit. Pages are an eclectic mix of odd images and too-subtle links or hot spots. In most cases you have to hunt for the link to the next page; in others you might just give up entirely.

2

In places it's easy to lose track of the focus of the site. At other times it transfixes you with its anarchistic 1970s style, reminiscent of early French film-noir directors, Truffaut, Godard, and Chabrol.

150

1

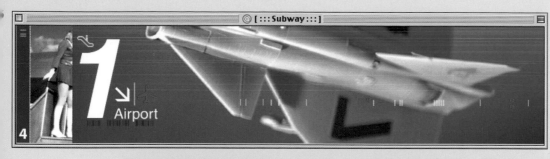

6 | 7 | 8 | 9 | 10

I get the feeling that Elixir has deliberately added a degree of obtuseness to its site. It's sort of a challenge: "Get in if you can. If you can't, then we probably didn't want your business in the first place."

151

3 | 4 | 5

Pop-up interaction is the main flavor with this engaging French site— although what pops up and why is, sometimes, a matter to fill another chapter!

GLASS ONION

Sydney-based Glass Onion is primarily a Web design company specializing in animation and Flash-empowered sites. Its home site, www.glassonion.com.au, is impressive for its complete interactivity: you can pre-select the viewing style (from CPU speeds and volume to connection type) and float through a range of interactive Shockwave animations designed for the curious and the information-hungry.

Glass Onion's client list reads like a *Who's Who* of the Australian entertainment and media world and includes a substantial folio of high-end animation credits with the Web site providing examples. Macromedia Shockwave is a prerequisite for quality viewing.

1

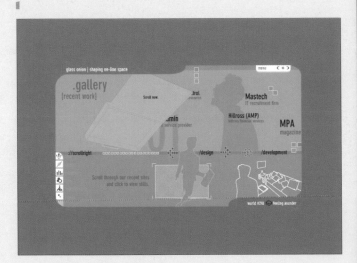

2
Although principally a Web development and design company, Glass Onion also produces animations for TV and broadband Internet. This is its oddball animation index page featuring animated buttons and moving levers that "stick" to the mouse as it passes close by.

2

1 | 3 | 4

The Glass Onion site features Flash technology with innovative graphics, very fast-loading data, and a feedback mechanism that allows you to customize the way the site reacts to the software you are using.

Click here to get the plug in

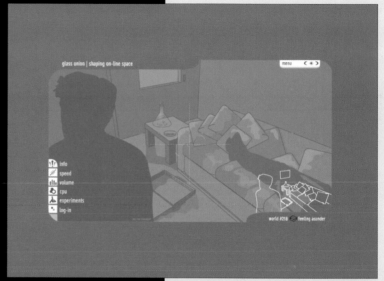

3

4

GMUNK

Defying description with its intricate and often obscure design metaphors and navigation style, www.gmunk.com is more an immersive adventure than a business site for a professional animator and Web designer.

Text and graphics are violently thrown together in a mish-mash of animatics, sound, and motion. It's a fine example of the capabilities of what can be done using Macromedia ShockWave on the Internet, and it's intriguing enough to lure you back for a second look.

The site contains numerous image maps and intriguing rollovers that are used to amuse and entertain rather than to educate or navigate. Finding your way round this site, therefore, is more a matter of luck than precision—but that's not its principal "raison d'etre."

1
Gmunk.com is one of the weirdest designer's sites on the Web. It can take ages to discover what this multilayered and circuitous site is all about.

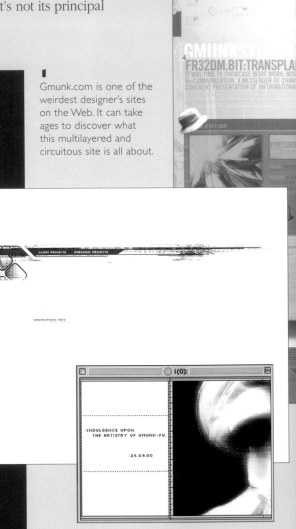

2 | 3

These are the client project pages, featuring animations with multiple pop-up windows. If you don't like the background music, you can dub your own from the selections provided.

4 | 5

Buttons and rollovers are small, dark, and mostly obscure on the home page but, once located, each clicks you through to entirely different visual and audio worlds.

THOMAS HERBRICH

Düsseldorf-based photographer/model maker Thomas Herbrich has created a simple yet effective site to promote his photographic and imaging skills. Click on the menu at www.herbrich.com and you move into the portfolio section containing his images. Click on any of the images to view a pop-up enlargement and select "How it was done" for a step-by-step account of the stages involved in creating each image. This is not a complex site, but it shows the work off to its best advantage. There are no fancy gimmicks, little animation other than a sliding menu bar along the top of the screen and a few dropdown text pages for those interested in learning about the photographer's services. Herbrich was making mechanical photo composites for more than 15 years before he took up electronic compositing as his medium.

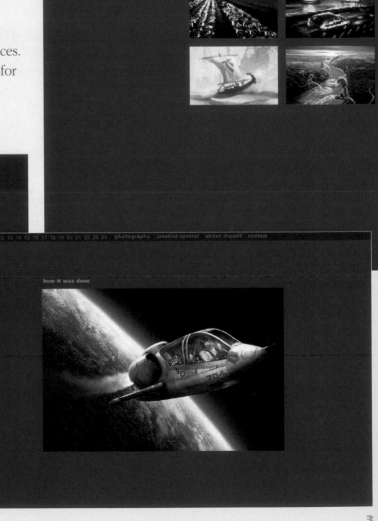

1 | 2
Herbrich's simple but well-designed site is light on gimmicks. The contents page is monotone, with few words. The photo section is a simple thumbnail layout, which in turn brings up a full-size photo.

156

1

2

3

4

157

5

3 | 4 | 5

If you look closely, you'll see that Herbrich is a model-maker as well as photographer, which explains the exceptional clarity of his images. It's good to see that not everything is done on a computer these days.

6

Each enlarged image has a "how it was done" link that explains the technique and thoughts behind that particular project.

I always look for scenes that contain an element of surprise. We know the world of spaceflight as a high-tech, clean and controlled affair - I wanted to design a radical and humorous opposite. Why shouldn't it be a run-down spaceship manned by a drunken pilot - and the man's even smoking!!! I always imagined this scene with a Russian cosmonaut - I didn't expect the Americans to have this kind of humour (or scrap).

Pay attention to the details. For example, there's a Playboy sticker, padlocks to secure the cockpit, and the pilot, schnapps and toilet paper in hand, looks to be on the way to a wild space party... "Boris", the cosmonaut, is played by my Brother Markus. The spaceship was originally an old helicopter that I took photographs of in a museum as a tourist in New York.

Incidentally, this photo was "borrowed" by Sony Music Taiwan for a CD cover.

6

LAND ROVER

The Australian site for Land Rover, www.landrover
.com.au, uses photographic imagery in an
unashamedly heroic light. Desktop as well as in-camera
special effects have been used extensively to create the
feeling of power, movement, style, and elegance
(depending on the model selected) throughout the site.
The site is rich in animation, image maps, image swaps,
rollovers, and animations designed to provide
information as much as to entertain. Complex image
montages are used throughout as wallpaper and texture,
reinforcing the themes of robustness, style, and adventure.

158

3

1

1 | 2
Land Rover's Australian
site combines rugged
imagery with some clever
Flash effects. The "Legend
of the Badge" animation
is a case in point,
featuring the brand's
high points in a moving
timeline animation. Even
if you are not into cars,
this is an interesting read.

2

3
Home page to perhaps
the most famous of all
recreational vehicle
manufacturers, Land
Rover has sites in many
countries around the
globe, although the
Australian site is perhaps
the most effective.

4

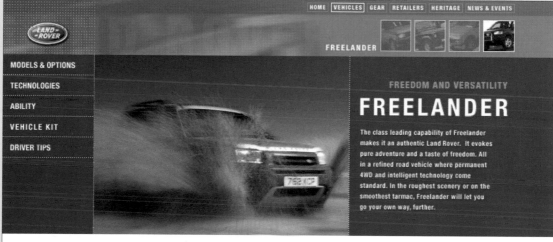

5

4 | 5 | 6
It's curious to see the
evolution of product
photography move from
the sterile-looking
"everything-in-sharp-
focus" style of the 1980s
to the more moody style
of the new millennium—
now the photography
is there to create an
impression of lifestyle and
not necessarily to present
itself in the greatest detail.

NATIONAL GEOGRAPHIC

National Geographic's Web site, www.national geographic.com, is notable for its simple and uncluttered use of high-quality images and text. The background for the images presented in features and in the gallery is usually white. A single image is used to capture your attention, while the text enhances and expands understanding of each story. Images are laid out in a row or column for simple navigation—similar to the frames in a roll of film. You also have the option to enlarge specific images for closer inspection, to zoom in for a look at the photographer's technical notes, or just move to other images and pages. This site remains typically "Geographic" in its "look" and "feel," yet it incorporates all the latest interactive Web enhancements.

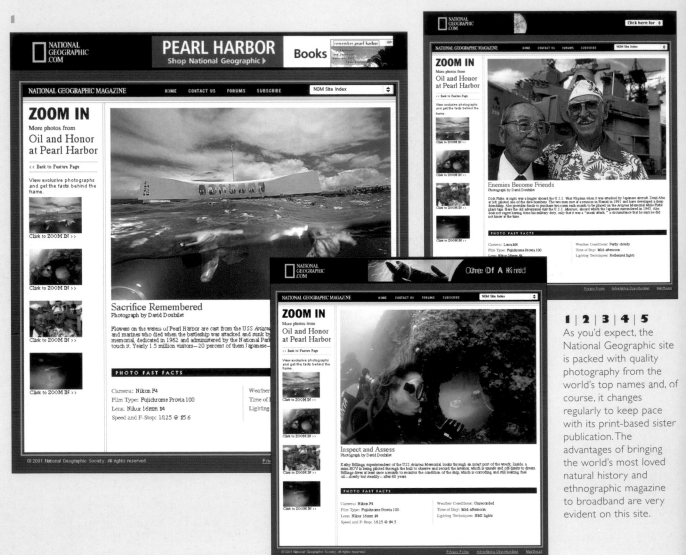

1 | 2 | 3 | 4 | 5

As you'd expect, the National Geographic site is packed with quality photography from the world's top names and, of course, it changes regularly to keep pace with its print-based sister publication. The advantages of bringing the world's most loved natural history and ethnographic magazine to broadband are very evident on this site.

7

6 | 7 | 8
You can access a huge wealth of video and audio data, making this one of the best all-round reference and general-interest sites on a well-photographed planet.

8

9
The "on assignment" pages add the photographers' perspective to the features, including some great anecdotal stories and incidental photography.

9

JOHNNIE WALKER

The Web site for the famous Johnnie Walker alcohol label oozes refinement, elegance, and history.

While www.scotch.com is a relatively small site by Internet standards, this boutique business lives up to the classy standard promoted by deluxe liquor makers: good product photography, beautiful graphics, a sense of history, and more.

Even the fonts used throughout the site have been meticulously chosen to fit in with the client's heritage and sense of place.

Images of the distilleries, the countryside, and even the graphics for the product labels say "class." It's a cohesive piece of design and Web building. There are few bells and whistles, but this site does not need such adrenaline to promote its peat-flavored products.

1
The entry page to scotch.com looks almost good enough to, well, drink!

2 | 3 | 4 | 5 | 6 | 7 | 8
Location photographs featuring distilleries and hints of local color are presented in a seductively somber desaturated coloration—

evocative of times past and emphasizing the fact that it takes years to produce something that's even remotely drinkable!

SINGLE MALT

Oban
Talisker
Lagavulin
Glenkinchie
Cragganmore
Dalwhinnie

BLENDED

Johnnie Walker
~ Red Label
~ Black Label
~ Gold Label
~ Blue Label

...ve taken the first step on a journey of ...very...here you'll experience the finest ...Scotland - and Scotch Whisky - has to offer.

7

The golden spirit of Skye

Talisker®, the Golden Spirit of Skye, is a turbulent Gaelic malt ; the only single malt from a spectacularly beautiful island of wild moorlands and dramatic mountain peaks. Sip Talisker and savour the bold marine influences of the Island of Skye.

Age & Strength: 10 Years, 45.8% alcohol by volume
Producing Region: Highland; Island
Distillery Address: Talisker Distillery, Carbost, Isle of Skye IV47 8SR

Tasting Notes

Color: deep gold, Nose: slightly sweet, phenolic and sea loch - a big island aroma, Body: full, well-balanced and round, Palate: a robust, smooth balance of smoke, salt, spices, malt and wood, Finish: long and deep. Peppery, peaty and salty, with a profound Hebridean depth and afterglow.

8

Johnnie Walker Red Label

Compared with other blended Scotch Whiskies in its category, Red Label's flavor has a distinctive and vibrant character. This is derived from blending the unique characteristics of single malt whiskies from some of Scotland's best distilleries. Cardhu®, for example, from the Speyside region, is the single malt whisky which forms the heart of the Red Label blend. Talisker®, on the Isle of Skye, lends Red Label its distinctive, complex, and slightly marine character. Whiskies from the Isle of Islay, such as Lagavulin, provide smoky complexity. In all, there are over forty single malt and aged grain whiskies which compose Johnnie Walker's famous Red Label blend.

The heritage of Johnnie Walker blended whiskies dates to 1820 when John Walker opened a provisions shop in Kilmarnock, Scotland and began selling Scotch Whisky. John Walker made a name for himself by mastering the art of blending single malt whiskies from distilleries all across Scotland to create a product of highest quality, infinitely greater than the sum of the individual component whiskies. John Walker handed down his knowledge and skill to his heirs, and thus began the House of Walker, the Scotch Whisky dynasty which helped create and shape the world's Scotch Whisky trade.

4

The gentle spirit with a warm heart

Dalwhinnie®, the Central Highland malt, is known as The Gentle Spirit with the Warm Heart. Located high on the wind-swept moors of the Grampian mountains, this exposed and remote distillery produces a surprisingly gentle whisky. To steal a line from Robert Burns, a sip is 'like a melody that's sweetly played in tune.'

Age & Strength: 15 Years, 43% alcohol by volume
Producing Region: Central Highlands
Distillery Address: Dalwhinnie Distillery, Dalwhinnie, Inverness-shire, PH19 1AB

Tasting Notes

Color: yellow gold, Nose: fruity aromatic, Body: round and full, Palate: begins with a light taste, clean and mellow, building to a smooth Highland glory - a balanced medley of malty sweetness, fruit and oak, with distinct whiffs of smoke, Finish: smooth, silky and heather honey.

5

The Lord of the Isles

Lagavulin®, the Islay single malt and Lord of the Isles, is her rich, robust song in peat. Sip a mere drop of Lagavulin at first and let its powerful bouquet embrace you.

Age & Strength: 16 years, 43% alcohol by volume
Producing Region: Islay
Distillery Address: Lagavulin Distillery, Port Ellen, Isle of Islay, Argyllshire PA42 7DU

Tasting Notes

Color: deep gold, Nose: heady and pungent with peat smoke, with a bit of salt, Body: full and rich, Palate: robust, dry flavor of peat dominates, with the tang of the sea surfacing occasionally, Finish: smooth, with a gentle bite to introduce the long, smoky afterglow of peat that lingers and warms the soul. glory.

6

Johnnie Walker Gold Label

Johnnie Walker Gold Label® is an inspired blend with a full-bodied yet refined taste, a creamy, balanced flavour and a lasting finish. It is a skilful fusion of just 15 of Scotland's rarest, most renowned whiskies, each matured at least then 18 years.

All 15 whiskies help build up the full orchestration of the blend, each contributing their special flavour and character. However a select few comprise the 'heart' of the Gold Label blend. The rare and highly prized Clynelish impart the honeyed creamy flavour and unique heather-lush. Royal Lochnagar provides the richness and a light, smoky nose. Cardhu, prized for its full body and silky smoothness is the foundation of all Walker blends, and Talisker contributes a real depth of flavor.

The heritage of Johnnie Walker blended whisky... dates to 1820 when John Walker opened a provisions shop in Kilmarnock, Scotland and began selling Scotch Whisky. John Walker made a name for himself by mastering the art of blending single malt whiskies from distilleries all across Scotland to create a product of highest quality, infinitely greater than the sum of the individual component whiskies. John Walker handed down his knowledge and skill to his heirs, and thus began the House of Walker, the Scotch Whisky dynasty which helped create and shape the world's Scotch Whisky trade.

LIQUORMART

Liquormart's splash page at www.liquormart.com.au is simply laid out against a clean-colored background. A brown paper bag sits under a lineup of five bottles representing the different sales lines: liqueurs, wines, beers, sparkling wines, and spirits. Clicking and dragging the bottle for the type of alcohol you like into the paper bag takes you to the page dealing with

information on those products. It's a fun splash page and a neat device for navigating into the rest of the site.

Each page uses a starter image to create a mood and association for the product, be it romantic (sparkling wines), stylish (spirits), or more down-to-earth and fun-loving (beer). This is an image-rich site full of quality photographic material blended into the overall design.

1 | 2
The opening page is a great example of a simple, visually based intuitive navigational structure.

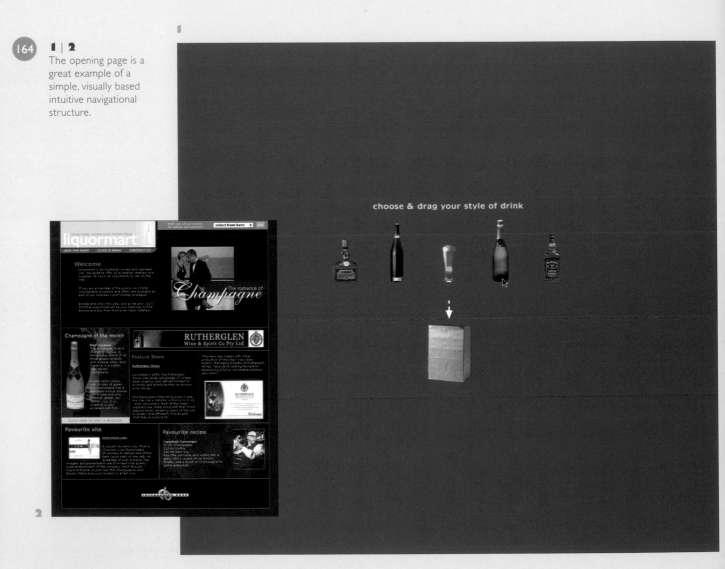

3 | 4 | 5 | 6
Though navigation is
straightforward, each
page is packed with rich
content and interesting
links to related sites.
You can find a wealth
of information about
brands, products, and
specials you never
realized you needed in
the first place!

ABSOLUT

The Absolut site at www.absolut.com is visual, strong, dynamic, and packed with page after page of multimedia entertainment. Oh, and it also advertises vodka through its award-winning photographic style and iconography. Thanks to the power of Macromedia ShockWave and the site designers, you can make your own movies, dub your own records, and do lots of completely un-vodka-related activities. It is a thrill to surf through this accomplished and exquisite piece of Web design. As a style statement, this is about the best you are ever likely to see on the Web.

166

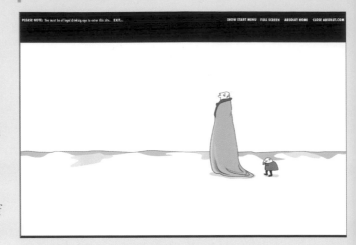

1

1 | 2
There's not much you can say about a spirit that's colorless and almost tasteless, so the designers have added an incredible degree of entertainment to the site —such as this weird Flash animated introduction.

3

3
This is the main page to absolut.com. Though it's a feast of potential activity, it has little connection with the appreciation and consumption of vodka— but who cares, it's fun!

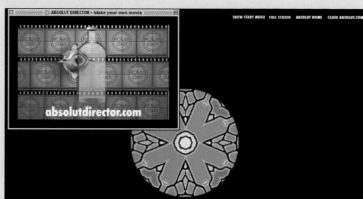

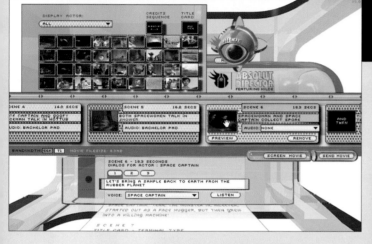

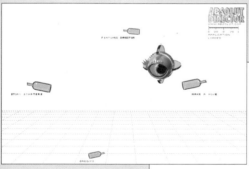

click the bottle to start.

4 | 5 | 6 | 7 | 8 | 9
Absolut.com offers the
visitor a brilliant array of
things to do, stopping just
short of offering samples
online (although I'm sure
that it's only a matter of
time). You can mix your
own music, check out a
great range of pop art,
watch or download
movies—you can even
make your own
(animated) movies.

6

MAJESTIC

Have no illusions, the world is treading the path to anarchy, or so the designers of this UK site might lead you to believe: www.majestic.ea.com is a futuristic game site designed to draw you deep into its alternative universe.

The site employs a range of provocative images combined in a futuristic, military-style dossier format. This is unashamedly a fun site using its multimedia power to add credence to the excitement, mystery, and appeal that the site designers are forecasting.

168

1 | 2 Definitely a boys' Web site, Majestic offers thrills and fabricated intrigue to anyone with a wet weekend to waste online. This site is filled with military-style images and militaristic iconography.

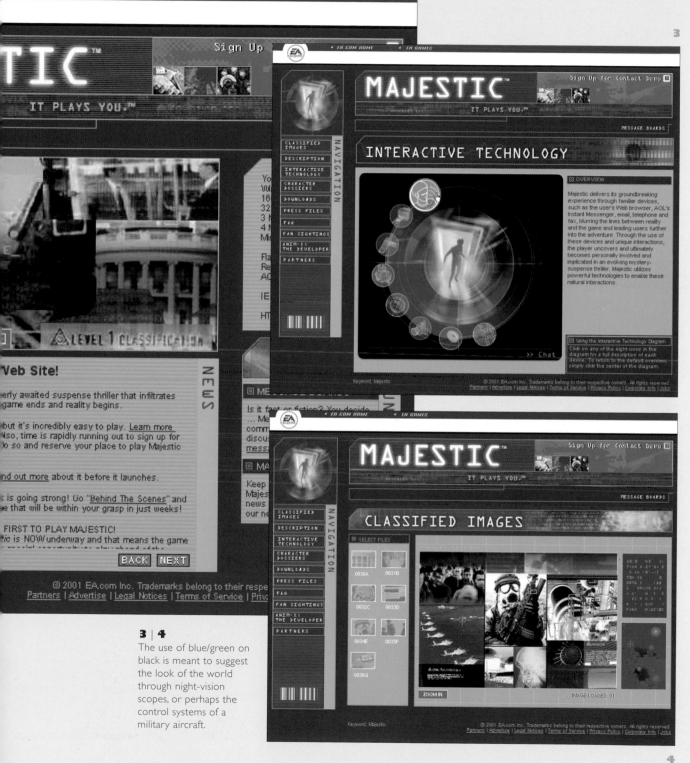

MAJESTIC™

IT PLAYS YOU.™

Sign Up for Contact Demo

MESSAGE BOARDS

NAVIGATION

CLASSIFIED IMAGES
DESCRIPTION
INTERACTIVE TECHNOLOGY
CHARACTER DOSSIERS
DOWNLOADS
PRESS FILES
FAQ
FAN SIGHTINGS
ANIM-X: THE DEVELOPER
PARTNERS

INTERACTIVE TECHNOLOGY

OVERVIEW

Majestic delivers its groundbreaking experience through familiar devices, such as the user's Web browser, AOL's Instant Messenger, email, telephone and fax, blurring the lines between reality and the game and leading users further into the adventure. Through the use of these devices and unique interactions, the player uncovers and ultimately becomes personally involved and implicated in an evolving mystery-suspense thriller. Majestic utilizes powerful technologies to enable these natural interactions.

Using the Interactive Technology Diagram
Click on any of the eight icons in the diagram for a full description of each device. To return to the default overview, simply click the center of the diagram.

>> Chat

Keyword: Majestic

© 2001 EA.com Inc. Trademarks belong to their respective owners. All rights reserved.
Partners | Advertise | Legal Notices | Terms of Service | Privacy Policy | Corporate Info | Jobs

CLASSIFIED IMAGES

SELECT FILES

0030A 0031B
0032C 0033D
0034E 0035F
0036G

ZOOM IN

...IMAGE LOADED: 01

Keyword: Majestic

© 2001 EA.com Inc. Trademarks belong to their respective owners. All rights reserved.
Partners | Advertise | Legal Notices | Terms of Service | Privacy Policy | Corporate Info | Jobs

3 | 4

The use of blue/green on black is meant to suggest the look of the world through night-vision scopes, or perhaps the control systems of a military aircraft.

4

TONIC

The site www.tonicuk.com has been included because the designers have created a striking mix of vector graphics with original photography and advanced interactive features. Access to this predominantly Flash site is made via image maps and mouse-overs—visitors enter the store in a swish of vector and bitmap graphics. Mousing around the 360-degree interior view allows you to select a range of apparel for closer inspection; you can check out the prices, and even click on the "security camera" to get a Webcam broadcast of what's happening in the shop! Cool stuff from Portobello Road, London.

Tonic
291 Portobello Road
London
W10 5TD

020 8962 0404

info@tonicuk.com

copyright © 2001 Tonic Ltd

view privacy statement | enter your email address to sign up for the tonic newslette

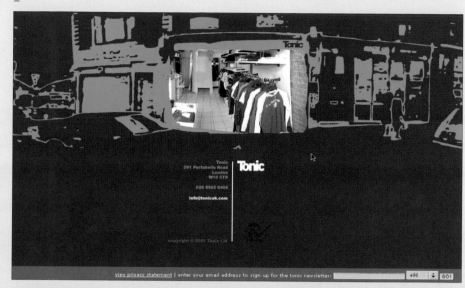

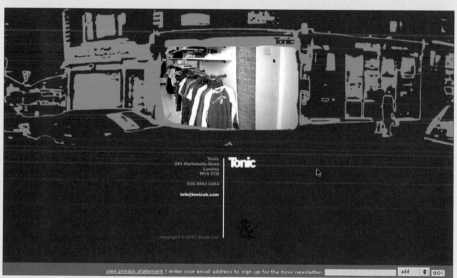

1

Tonic's hip Web site has a number of interesting customer-magnets that include a customer-cam and a cute Flash intro.

2 | 3

The design of this site makes extensive use of QuickTime VR technology, permitting you to zoom in on store details and even to become the instore security camera! You still can't try on the shoes, though!

ASTON MARTIN

Like many of the auto sites, www.astonmartin.com is a visual exercise in combining great motoring photography with a range of neat Flash technology. The Aston Martin site helps to cultivate a motoring image that would appeal to any "wanna-be" James Bonds.

The site is minimalist in design, featuring well laid-out graphics and images. Clicking on the Aston Martin logo reveals the page layout image in all its full glory. A clever design device. The site also opens with an elegant pastiche of the company history in images.

Like most car sites, this is target-driven and the look is consciously masculine.

The recurring use of curved lines and the color combination of British racing green and white works to keep the design of this site a unified whole.

1 | 2 | 3
The Aston Martin Web site conveys a feeling of opulence, from its Flash-enhanced opening sequence to its simple but effective menu page. Many of the images are presented in sumptuous duotones to great effect.

Aston Martin Image Gallery
DB7 Coupe

Download 800 x 600
Download 1024 x 768

10 | 11 | 12
The high quality of the photography helps to lend the Aston Martin website a sense of opulence and class, exactly how you are meant to think of the company's product. Note how the images are set at an angle to suggest a sense of movement.

173

4

5

6

7

8

11

12

9

4 | 5 | 6 | 7 | 8 | 9
The Aston Martin logo itself is a comment on power and status— and though the intro is animated, it hardly needs to be, such is the strength of the brand.

NELSON-ATKINS MUSEUM OF ART

A Web version of an exhibition held at Missouri's Nelson-Atkins Museum of Art, Tempus Fugit is a joy to behold because of its arresting and stylish imagery and its faultless treatment of color and text.

The site www.nelson-atkins.org/tempusfugit/ is Flash-enabled, but its real success lies in the depiction and presentation of images with a graphic simplicity that complements the subject matter remarkably well.

Enter the site and learn, interactively, about the museum, its exhibition *Tempus Fugit* (Time Flies), plus what it is doing to preserve its treasures and how it uses technology to discover more than the eye or history can reveal. Visitors can access a range of visual effects, from extreme closeup views of some of the exhibits to neat map navigation devices that take you round the exhibition (and the site).

174

1 | 2 | 3
This site works because of its selection and arrangement of truly beautiful images sourced from the worlds of fine art, painting, and sculpture. Note how the designers have cropped the images for interesting effect.

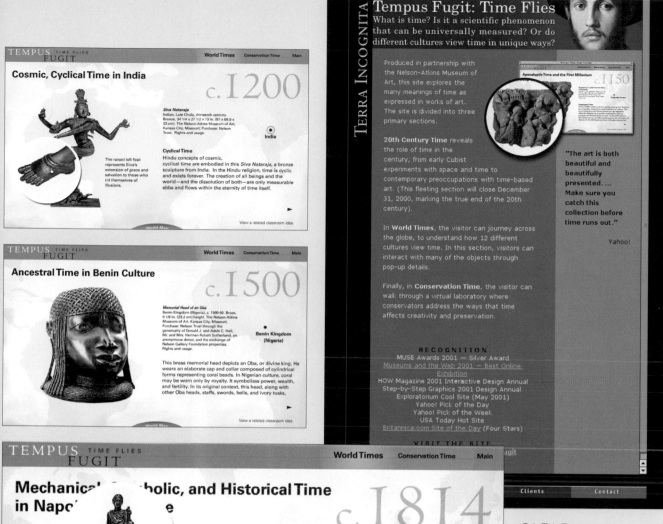

Tempus Fugit: Time Flies

What is time? Is it a scientific phenomenon that can be universally measured? Or do different cultures view time in unique ways?

Produced in partnership with the Nelson-Atkins Museum of Art, this site explores the many meanings of time as expressed in works of art. The site is divided into three primary sections.

20th Century Time reveals the role of time in the century, from early Cubist experiments with space and time to contemporary preoccupations with time-based art. (This fleeting section will close December 31, 2000, marking the true end of the 20th century).

In **World Times**, the visitor can journey across the globe, to understand how 12 different cultures view time. In this section, visitors can interact with many of the objects through pop-up details.

Finally, in **Conservation Time**, the visitor can walk through a virtual laboratory where conservators address the ways that time affects creativity and preservation.

RECOGNITION
MUSE Awards 2001 — Silver Award
Museums and the Web 2001 — Best Online Exhibition
HOW Magazine 2001 Interactive Design Annual
Step-by-Step Graphics 2001 Design Annual
Exploratorium Cool Site (May 2001)
Yahoo! Pick of the Day
Yahoo! Pick of the Week
USA Today Hot Site
Britannica.com Site of the Day (Four Stars)

VISIT THE SITE

"The art is both beautiful and beautifully presented. ... Make sure you catch this collection before time runs out."

Yahoo!

175

4 | 5 | 6
Like all good educational sites, Tempus Fugit is packed with stuff—some relevant and some perhaps not so—but it's all interesting even to the casual browser.

7
One of the credits for Tempus Fugit goes to another site of note, Terra Incognita, featured on pages 182 and 183.

INTERNET CAR COMPANY

An unusual approach to selling cars online is found at Internet Car's "virtual" showroom at www.netcarco .co.uk. Virtual selling has been around for some years, but this site is a great exposition for the technology.

You can view the site in normal mode, but there's also a good degree of interactivity—especially in the best-sellers section and the virtual showroom. Click on the car of your dreams and take a 180-degree tour around the seating, the dashboard, the interior and exterior details for that vehicle. Image maps lead you to any color choices, vehicle specifications, add-ons, and accessories available. It's a fun easy-to-use site and (probably) a good place from which to buy a car.

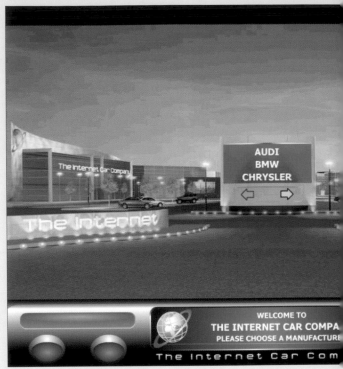

1 | 2
I have no idea if this is a successful site or not—after all, the thought of spending so much hard-earned cash without actually being able to sit in or try out the product is scary, to say the least.

3 | 4
The Internet Car Company allows you to view specific car models in great detail, both inside and out.

5 | 6 | 7 | 8 | 9
The left-hand group shows the virtual car showroom, with a selected model on the (rotatable) podium and a VR representation of its interior in the lower screen. You can start the engine, close the door, and sound the horn, if that's what turns you on.

10
The VR screen at the base of each showroom page allows visitors to check details such as interior layout, and even to choose the upholstery color, while keeping a beady eye on the price.

MICHAEL HALFORD

The home page for designer/imager Michael Halford at www.netspace.net.au/~inu demonstrates the necessity for a powerful, yet simple splash page.

Halford uses simple eye-catching symbols. The site is not complex or deep, just gutsy and quick to access.

It works well, and the symbols and images remain in the memory long after you have moved on. Short, sharp, simple, and very effective. Despite displaying vibrant and striking imagery, it would be good to see how the works are used in commercial environments.

2

178

1 | 2
Michael Halford's index page is simple and to the point. Mouse-click one of the head icons and move to the gallery or the résumé.

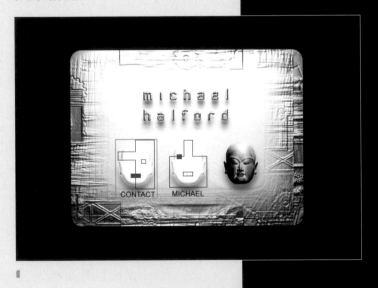

1

detail 50%
detail 100%
back

3 | 4 | 5
Click the image for a close-up view of a particular artwork, or click again for a 200% zoom-in, for a worm's-eye view of the canvas. Simple but highly effective.

1

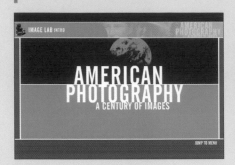

2

3

11

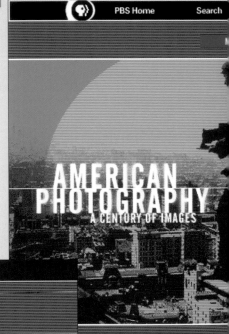

180

The site www.pbs.org/ktca/americanphotography is a celebration of 100 years of American photography in images and moving pictures. The US being a nation that actively supports photography and the arts, the site is packed with fine images and informative text. Check out the Image Lab, an interactive ShockWave-driven interface that offers opinions on how image cropping effects the final result, how digital manipulation alters the perception of an image, and a short introduction on the making of a classic image.

10 | 11
Sections include "Photography and War," plus the poignant "Digital Truth" section describing how images can be used to create an illusion for a range of reasons—good and not so good.

10

12
Photos can lie. This 1991 photo purported to show three US pilots imprisoned in North Vietnam. It was widely believed, until another startlingly similar image was found dating from the Russian Revolution.

4

5

6

7

8

9

1 | 2 | 3 | 4 | 5 | 6 | 7 | 8 | 9

One of the real fun parts of this site is the ShockWave-enhanced "Image Lab" section, which shows you, among other things, how new technologies have enabled the meaning, or the way we read images, to be radically changed, for political or economic reasons. It's entertaining and provides a fascinating insight into how easy it is to manipulate images to suit almost any situation, political or otherwise.

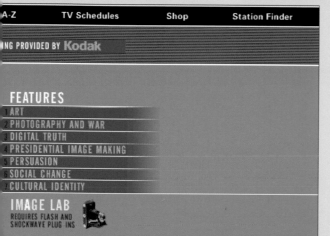

A-Z   TV Schedules   Shop   Station Finder

...NG PROVIDED BY **Kodak**

FEATURES

1 ART
2 PHOTOGRAPHY AND WAR
3 DIGITAL TRUTH
4 PRESIDENTIAL IMAGE MAKING
5 PERSUASION
6 SOCIAL CHANGE
7 CULTURAL IDENTITY

IMAGE LAB
REQUIRES FLASH AND
SHOCKWAVE PLUG INS.

THE FILM AND MORE
TEACHER'S GUIDE
SHOP PBS
LINKS SEEN ON TV
FEEDBACK

PHOTO CREDITS

ts, The Arthur Vin...

AMERICAN PHOTOGRAPHY
A CENTURY OF IMAGES

▶ FEATURES   ▶ IMAGE LAB   ▶ HOME

DIGITAL TRUTH

It is true that *The National Geographic* moved two of the Egyptian pyramids closer together on a cover, to fit the vertical format. And, yes, the cover photo on *A Day in the Life of America* was manipulated to move the cowboy closer to the moon, again to fit the format.

Does that mean photographic truth is at an end? Who says it ever existed? Photographs have always been manipulated. Usually the results have not been big whopper lies, pictures that claimed something happened when it didn't, but less serious sins, touch-ups in ads and portraits. The tabloids have always used a bag of photographic tricks. In early examples, as when cameras were barred from courtrooms, scenes were staged and images created through cutting and pasting to show what happened. The tabloids still use

◉ Vietnam Vets/Soviet Farmers

...surfaced that supposedly showed three American Vietnam pilots

12

TERRA INCOGNITA

Terra Incognita is a multimedia design company that has been involved in a number of interesting Web projects—notably for clients such as the National Geographic and the Smithsonian Institute in the US.

The site www.terraincognita.com proves that you do not need Flash, streaming video, and other "bells and whistles" to make an impact when beautiful images and careful design will do the job. Placement, position, and a contrast of images and design elements are well balanced as you surf through its many pages, covering a wide range of ethnological subject matter. Each individual project seems to have picked up considerable airtime and awards for design, creativity, and educational value. A recent exhibit for the Smithsonian is particularly good, with great use of iconography, symbolism, and image montaging in its headers, menus, and sidebars.

1
Terra Incognita's site is reminiscent of other, perhaps more famous sites, or is it because this company has had a hand in designing those very sites?

2 | 3
This is one of the company's many success stories: a timeline-style page taken from an online exhibition designed for the Smithsonian Institute.

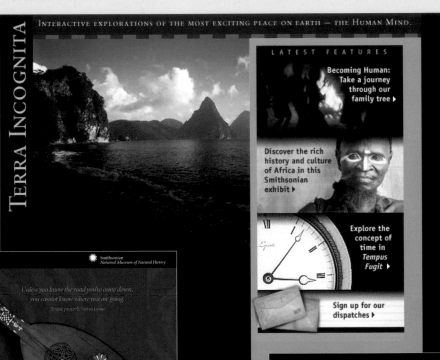

TERRA INCOGNITA

Becoming Human
Take a voyage through four million years of human evolution with Dr. Donald Johanson.....

This original documentary experience explores the question — What makes us human? Guided by Dr. Donald Johanson, who discovered the Lucy skeleton in 1974, guests can walk through a paleontological dig, meet scientists in the field, and trace the evolution of the hominid species over the last four million years. This site was produced in association with NeonSky Creative Media.

RECOGNITION
Scientific American SciTech Web Award
Exploratorium Cool Site
The Scout Report
Macromedia Site of the Day
USA Today Hot Site
Yahoo! Pick of the Day
Yahooligans! Cool Site

VISIT THE SITE
www.becominghuman.org

"This site, probably the best online documentary seen by this reviewer, should appeal to anyone with an interest in human origins and is highly recommended. "

— Michael de Nie
The Scout Report
April 20, 2001

Becoming Human
Take a voyage through four million years of human evolution with Dr. Donald Johanson.....

Clients ▶ Institute of Human Origins

Main   Company   Clients   Contact

4 | 5 | 6
It's good to see a site that uses such a range of textures, logos, and colorful design elements without losing the plot totally. This style is normally the preserve of the "educational site," which this company designs—and designs well.

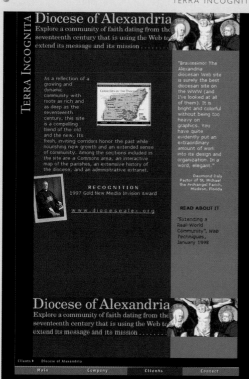

TERRA INCOGNITA

Diocese of Alexandria
Explore a community of faith dating from the seventeenth century that is using the Web to extend its message and its mission . . . .

As a reflection of a growing and dynamic community with roots as rich and as deep as the seventeenth century, this site is a compelling blend of the old and the new. Its fresh, inviting corridors honor the past while nourishing new growth and an extended sense of community. Among the sections included in the site are a Commons area, an interactive map of the parishes, an extensive history of the diocese, and an administrative extranet.

RECOGNITION
1997 Gold New Media Invision Award

www.diocesealex.org

"Bravissimo! The Alexandria diocesan Web site is surely the best diocesan site on the WWW (and I've looked at all of them). It is bright and colorful without being too heavy on graphics. You have quite evidently put an extraordinary amount of work into its design and organization. In a word, elegant."

Desmond Daly
Pastor of St. Michael the Archangel Parish, Hudson, Florida

READ ABOUT IT
"Extending a Real-World Community", Web Techniques, January 1998

Diocese of Alexandria
Explore a community of faith dating from the seventeenth century that is using the Web to extend its message and its mission . . . .

Clients ▶   Diocese of Alexandria

Main   Company   Clients   Contact

183

TERRA INCOGNITA

African Voices
Join the Smithsonian for an exploration of Africa's rich history and culture. . . .

This large-scale online exhibition compliments the new African cultures hall of the Smithsonian's National Museum of Natural History. Like the physical exhibit, the site tells the story of life in Africa using a wide range of engaging multimedia content. Among the highlights of this extensive site include: an interactive timeline of African history, a lively (and noisy) recreation of an African marketplace, personal accounts of daily life in Africa, and dozens of photos and objects from the exhibition.

"An abundance of enlightening and interactive features with highly impressive design and navigation. African Voices is an outstanding Internet showcase that truly does justice to the countries it represents."

— Britannica.com

READ MORE ABOUT IT
"A Walk Through an Online Exhibit" Web Techniques, July 2000

"The Smithsonian Institution's 'African Voices'" cybercoverage, July 25, 2001

RECOGNITION
Best of Show — HOW Magazine
2001 Interactive Design Annual
Step-by-Step Graphics 2001 Design Annual
Yahoo! Pick of the Day
USA Today Hot Site
Britannica.com Site of the Day (four stars)

VISIT THE SITE
www.mnh.si.edu/africanvoices

Clients ▶   National Museum of Natural History

Main   Company   Clients   Contact

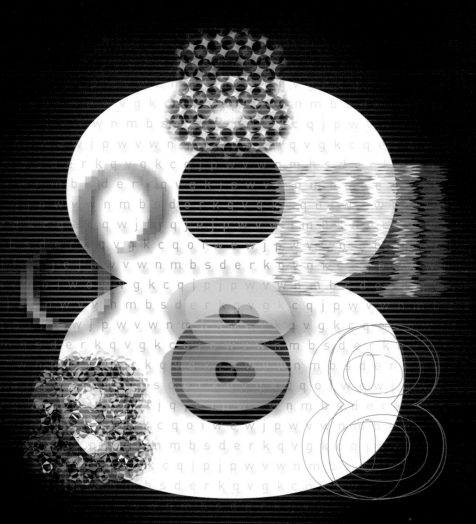

GLOSSARY

Adobe Acrobat A proprietary "portable document format" (PDF) file that has fonts and pictures embedded in the document, enabling it to be viewed and printed on different computer systems.

analog Short for "analogous" or "similar to," the use of signals or information processed by a physical variation such as light or voltage, as distinct from digital signals. Sound, photographs, and some video are examples of Web components whose native form is analog and therefore need to be converted to digital form before they can be used on the Web.

animation The process by which a sequence of images, displayed in quick succession, is used to show motion. In the Web context, there are essentially two different types of animation—two-dimensional and three-dimensional. Different creation programs are required for each type. In addition, if the animation is to be used on a Website, then the final files must be ported to a format that is suitable for net use.

antialias/antialiasing A technique of optically eliminating the jagged effect of bitmapped images or text reproduced on low-resolution devices such as monitors. This is achieved by blending the color at the edges of the object with its background by averaging the density of the range of pixels involved.

assets These refer to the different components that make up a functioning Website. These may include text, images, animation, movies, buttons, text, and sound. Designing and producing Websites is a complex process primarily because so many different skills and technologies are involved in the creation of the site's assets. Complex, or particularly large, sites require strict control over the storage of assets.

authoring This is a generic term used to describe the process by which multimedia, or interactive Web environments, are created. Authoring programs are pieces of software that allow producers to put together a variety of assets in one information product. Most Web authoring programs are called page layout or Website construction packages.

bandwidth This refers to the amount of information that can flow through a connection between the Internet and a computer in a given period of time. Most home computers connect via a modem and the public telephone system. This is the slowest form of connection and a lot of users now prefer to use the faster service provided by cable, or DSL connections.

banner The advertisements that often span the top or bottom sections of Web pages. As the hosting companies restrict the size of files that can be used as banners, these advertisements are often good examples of how to squeeze the most dynamic results out of the smallest files.

bit A commonly used acronym for binary digit, the smallest piece of information a computer can use. A bit is expressed as one of two values—a 1 or a 0, on or off.

bit depth The number of bits assigned to each pixel on a monitor, scanner, or image file. Most systems can now handle 24 bit, or up to 16.7 million, colors. In contrast, the GIF file format can only support eight-bit color, or 256 different hues.

bitmap A bitmap is a "map" describing the location and binary state of "bits" that define a complete collection of pixels or dots that comprise an image. Sometimes this term is also used to refer to pictures that only have black and white pixels.

brightness The strength of luminescence from light to dark.

browser An application that is used to access the World Wide Web across the Internet. The most widely used browsers are Microsoft's Internet Explorer and Netscape's Navigator. There are differences between the way that browsers display Web pages.

CMYK Color model describing the primary colors of reflective light: cyan (C), magenta (M), and yellow (Y). Together with black (K), they are used in most forms of printing. The letter K is used rather than B to avoid confusion with blue.

CODEC Acronym for compression/ decompression. Many assets used in Web production are data-heavy. In order that these

components can be downloaded quickly when used as part of a Web page, a form of CODEC is used to shrink the size of the files. For example, with pictures, the JPEG compression algorithm is used, whereas for movie files, something like MPEG compression may be employed to shrink big files.

content The content of a Website refers to a combination of text, images, and other assets that make up the information contained on the pages of the site. A Web page layout program is used to manipulate and control the positioning of this content.

cross platform The term applied to software or Websites that may be run or viewed on different computer systems. Web designers should concentrate on making sure that their applications are compatible with both Macintosh and Windows based systems, as these two platforms are used by the majority of the world's Web audience.

desaturate To reduce the purity of a color, thus making it grayer.

digital watermark An invisible "marker" added to an image to identify it as the owner's property.

dithering A technique of "interpolation" that calculates the average value of adjacent pixels. This technique is most often used to add extra pixels to an image—to smooth an edge, for example, or to simulate a large range of hues.

e-commerce Commercial transactions conducted electronically over a network or the Internet. This area of Web design is very specialized and requires in-depth understanding of secure protocols and financial transactions technology.

embedding This is a technique whereby external files, usually video, animation, or sound files, are incorporated into a Web page. If the browser supports the files natively, then the embedding process is merely a way of including a reference to the file in the HTML code. If, on the other hand, there is no native support, then the embedding process can also include notifying the viewer that a specialist plug-in is required to play, or view the file.

EPS (Encapsulated PostScript) A standard file format that includes all the PostScript data necessary to display and reproduce images in many graphics and layout programs.

feathering A similar process to antialiasing, this blurs the edge pixels of a selection to give a soft border.

File Transfer Protocol (FTP) A standard system for transmitting files between computers across the Internet or a network. Most Web page production programs construct pages and sites locally on the machine situated on the designer's desk. When the project is finished, the completed site is then uploaded to a Web server. An FTP program is used to transfer the files from where they are stored on the local machine to the Web server.

file format The particular method used to store the digital data that makes up a computer file. Some file formats like TIFF, JPEG, and WAV can be read by many different programs, while others, such as the Photoshop format PSD, are designed for use with an single piece of software.

FireWire An Apple-developed technology that allows high-speed communications between the computer and peripherals such as external hard drives and digital cameras.

Flash Software for creating vector graphics and animations for Web presentations. Flash generates small files that are correspondingly quick to download and, being vector, are scalable to any dimension without an increase in file size.

form A special type of Web page that provides users with the means to input information directly into the Website. Form pages are often used to collect information about viewers, or as a way of collecting password and username data before allowing access to secure areas.

frames These are a means of displaying more than one page at a time within a single window—the window is divided into separate areas ("frames"), each one displaying a different page. Each of the sections remain independent of each other even though visually they might appear to be a single entity.

FTP (file transfer protocol) A standard system for transmitting files between computers across the Internet or a network. Although Web browsers incorporate FTP capabilities, dedicated FTP applications provide greater flexibility.

gamma A measure of the contrast in a digital image, photographic film or paper, or processing technique. Gamma curves can be used within the software that may come with a scanner so that you can preset the amount of light and dark and contrast on input.

GIF The Graphics Interchange Format, or GIF, is a format designed specifically to produce very small, optimized image files for the Web. GIFs also provide basic inbuilt animation features. The format allows for simple transparency but can only contain up to 256 colors.

HSB A color model based on the variables of Hue, Saturation, and Brightness.

HTML (Hypertext Markup Language) A text-based "page description language" used to format documents published on the World Wide Web, and which can be viewed with Web browsers. Early Web design packages constructed pages by hard coding directly in HTML. The new generation of Web page design programs provide a visual front end to the coding process.

hue A color as found in its pure state in the spectrum.

hyperlink An embedded link between text, pictures, buttons in a Web page, and other parts of the site or another Website. Sometimes called a "hot link".

icon These are visual symbols used to represent a program, function, or button. In Web design, icons are most often used for the navigation system.

image map An image that contains a series of embedded links to other documents or Websites. These links are activated when clicked on in the appropriate area of the image.

interface This is a term most used to describe the screen design that links the user with the computer program or Website. The quality of the user interface often determines how well users will be able to navigate their way around the pages within the site.

Internet The entire collection of connected world-wide networks, including those used solely for the Web.

interpolation A computer calculation used to estimate unknown values that fall between known values. This process is used, for example, to redefine pixels in bitmapped images after they have been modified in some way, such as when an image is resized (called "resampling"), rotated, or if color corrections have been made.

intranet Unlike the Internet, this term refers to an internal or private network. Web pages can be posted to this internal network just as easily as if they were posted to the Web. Large companies often maintain a private Web presence on their intranet.

Java A programming language devised for creating small applications ("applets") that can be downloaded from a Web server and used, typically in conjunction with a Web browser to add dynamic effects such as animations.

JPEG This is a digital image file form format particularly suited to continuous-tone images such as photographs. It uses a lossy compression algorithm to squeeze large images into smaller, more compact files. The Joint Photographers Expert Group first created the format.

lossless / lossy Refers to data-losing qualities of different compression methods: lossless means that no image information is lost; lossy means that some (or much) of the image data is lost in the compression process.

metadata The metadata list at the top of most Web pages provides a summary of the information contained within those pages. Search engines often use metadata information as a way of categorizing and providing search references for sites.

MP3 An audio file format used to compress digital audio files by as much as 100 to 1. Most often used by music sites to give visitors the best possible sound while still taking into account the restrictions of Web delivery.

187

GLOSSARY

multimedia Multimedia is a generic term used to describe any combination of sound, video, animation, graphics, and text incorporated into a software product or presentation.

navigation system The system by which users navigate from one page of Website to another. It usually takes the form of a series of buttons.

palette This term refers to a subset of colors that are needed to display a particular image. For instance, a GIF image will have a palette containing a maximum of 256 individual and distinct colors.

PDF (Portable Document Format) a cross-platform format that allows complex, multifeatured documents to be created, retaining all text and picture formatting, then viewed and printed on any computer that has an appropriate "reader" installed.

plug-in Subsidiary software for a browser or other package that enables it to perform additional functions, e.g., play sound, movies, or video.

PostScript Adobe Systems Inc.'s proprietary "page description language" for image output to laser printers and high-resolution imagesetters.

resampling Altering an image by modifying pixels to either increase or decrease its resolution. Increasing the number of pixels is called "resampling up," while reducing the number is known as "resampling down" or "downsampling."

rollover button A graphic button type that changes in appearance when the mouse pointer moves over it.

saturation A variation in color of the same total brightness from nonc (gray) through pastel shades (low saturation) to pure (fully saturated) color with no gray.

search engine An indexing program that allows users to input search terms and locate a list of pages and Websites that contain a reference to the search item.

RAM (Random Access Memory) The memory "space" made available by the computer, into which some or all of an application's code is loaded and remembered while you work with it. Generally speaking, the more, the better. Imaging software such as Photoshop needs up to five times the size of the files that you are working on to process images.

RGB (Red Green Blue) The primary colors of the "additive" color model, used in video technology, computer monitors, and for graphics such as for the Web and multimedia that will not ultimately be printed by the four-color (CMYK) process method.

thumbnail A small version of a larger image, to which it is linked. When the visitor clicks the thumbnail, the larger image is downloaded and displayed, sometimes in a new window.

tile An image repeated two or more times to create a background. A background image, smaller than the size of the screen (which is, in turn, arbitrary), is automatically tiled to fill the screen.

URL (Uniform Resource Locator) The unique address of a page on the Web, comprising three elements: the protocol to be used (such as http), the domain name ("host"), and the directory name followed by pathnames to any particular file. URL is the formal term that refers to the Web address of a specific Website.

vector graphics A graphics file that uses mathematical descriptions of lines, curves, and angles. When using vector graphics, it does not matter how large or small you print the file, it will still reproduce perfectly because there are no bitmapped pixels.

websafe Color that will not be changed when an image is optimized for the Web.

WAV (Waveform) A digital audio file format that can be integrated into most multimedia and Web productions.

INDEX

WEB SITES FEATURED